THE MOSCOW NOTEBOOKS

OSIP MANDELSTAM

The Moscow Notebooks

TRANSLATED BY
RICHARD & ELIZABETH McKANE

BLOODAXE BOOKS

ISBN: 1 85224 126 8

First published 1991 by
Bloodaxe Books Ltd,
P.O. Box 1SN,
Newcastle upon Tyne NE99 1SN.

Bloodaxe Books Ltd acknowledges
the financial assistance of Northern Arts.

Typesetting by Bryan Williamson, Darwen, Lancashire.

Printed in Great Britain by
Bell & Bain Limited, Glasgow, Scotland.

For Peter Norman

Acknowledgements

For these translations we have used the American edition of Osip Mandelstam's *Complete Works*, edited by G.P. Struve and B.A. Filipoff, 4 vols (Inter Language Literary Associates, 1967-81). This edition of the *Moscow Notebooks* is the first to follow the order established by Nadezhda Mandelstam (from the so-called 'Vatican Codex' copied out in Voronezh and committed to paper as well as Nadezhda Mandelstam's memory).

Elizabeth and I were able to begin working on these translations together when I was awarded the Hodder Fellowship in the Humanities at Princeton University (1978-79). The Russian poets Victor Krivulin and Dmitri Vedenyapin made several valuable suggestions in Moscow and Leningrad where I had contributed to the Akhmatova and Pasternak Centenary conferences on trips partly funded by the British Council. There were also many useful suggestions from Irina Kuzminsky, who read the final manuscript. Jennifer Baines' book *Mandelstam: The Later Poetry* (Cambridge University Press, 1976) offered a unique perspective. But the most invaluable contribution was the sense of support and inspiration from our friend Peter Norman.   RMcK

Contents

*'Titles' in inverted commas are "contingency titles"
from first lines of poems untitled in Russian.*

SECOND MOSCOW NOTEBOOK

Introduction

Osip Mandelstam was born into a Jewish family in Warsaw on 15 January 1891. The family moved to Pavlovsk, outside St Petersburg, very soon after Osip's birth. St Petersburg, Petrograd, Leningrad, or simply Peter, was to be *his* city. After his wanderings in the Crimea, Armenia, Georgia, and after living in Moscow, he returned there in 1930, and said: 'I've returned to my city of childhood illnesses and tears,/the city, that I know like the veins on the back of my hand.' (MN. I.9).

Petersburg was the city of Pushkin, Dostoyevsky and Alexander Blok, and of Mandelstam's contemporaries, the great poets Mayakovsky, Gumilyov and Akhmatova. In 1900 he went to school there at the privileged Tenishev Lycée, where he studied Classics, Humanities and Russian literature. He was already writing poems as a schoolboy. In *The Noise of Time* (1925), Mandelstam left an impressionistic portrait of the city – and his childhood.

In October 1907, having finished the Tenishev Lycée, he was sent abroad by his parents to Paris, returning to Petersburg in the summer. In November of 1909 he went to Switzerland and then on to Italy. As a young man he subsequently made other trips abroad. He was also a frequent visitor to Finland.

He attended Petersburg University from 1912 to 1917, but never graduated. In the spring of 1910 he went to lectures and readings of poetry at the Symbolist poet Vyacheslav Ivanov's 'Tower', the meeting place for many of the great Russian poets-to-be. It was partly from these gatherings that the Acmeist movement emerged, in which Anna Akhmatova, her husband Nikolai Gumilyov and Osip Mandelstam played the major roles.

As a young man, Mandelstam seems to have combined a savage shyness, with outspokenness, physical ungainliness and eccentricity. But when he read his poetry at readings in Vyacheslav Ivanov's Tower, or at the Stray Dog Café – the centre in Petersburg in the early 1910s of the century for performance poetry and cabaret – the audience was spellbound.

Mandelstam's first book *Stone* was published in 1913. *Tristia* followed in 1922. There then was a gap before a collection *Poems 1921-1925* was published together with *Stone* and *Tristia* in 1928, the year when much of his prose and critical prose was published. It was his last publication to appear in book form in his country for over thirty years.

His battle with time (he hated clocks, "development" and progress) and with his times, was resolved in the context of the Judaeo-Christian-Hellenic tradition. He valued that tradition along with the values of the intelligentsia and nineteenth-century Russian literature. Ultimately he believed that his poetry would transcend the times.

When he started writing the *Moscow Notebooks* in October 1930, he was actually in Tiflis, Georgia. He had not written any poetry for over five years. A scandal over Mandelstam's editing of two translations of Charles de Coster's novel *Thyl Ulenspiegel*, involving unjust accusations of plagiarism, had prompted his vitriolic, therapeutic *Fourth Prose*, written in Armenia. The Armenian trip, which lasted for eight months in 1930, liberated the Mandelstams from Moscow. It was only possible because Mandelstam had a powerful ally in the Kremlin, Nikolai Bukharin (who was later purged). Another factor that goaded Mandelstam to write poetry again was Mayakovsky's suicide in April 1930, which he heard about in Armenia, and a further spur was his friendship with the biologist B.S. Kuzin: 'I was awoken by friendship as if by a gunshot.' (MN. II.11).

The Mandelstams returned to Leningrad, via Moscow, in November 1930. They were only able to stay there for four months, since they were blocked by Tikhonov of the Writers Union: 'Mandelstam will not live in Leningrad. We will not give him a room' and 'Let him go to Moscow. Leningrad writers don't want him here.' Mandelstam was finally to get a flat in the Furmanov backstreet in Moscow, having led a vagabond life in Moscow and the south. This flat moved Osip Mandelstam to write one of the most horrific poems on life in Moscow (MN. II.17).

After the publication of the Armenian Cycle in *Novy Mir* and *Journey to Armenia* in 1931 in *Zvezda*, with its thinly veiled attack on tyranny in the closing passages (the editor was sacked), Mandelstam was not to be published again in his lifetime.

However, although Mandelstam was not published, he still gave readings. At one such reading in Leningrad in 1933, he was asked what he thought about contemporary Russian poetry. With his eyes flashing, he replied: 'What answer do you want from me? I am the friend of my friends! I am the contemporary of Akhmatova!' The crowd burst into applause.

When Mandelstam was ready he took on his 'equal', as referred to in the last line of 'The Wolf' (MN. I.15). In the winter of 1933 he read the 'Epigram to Stalin' (MN. II.20), to several people. It was the beginning of his confrontation with Stalin, for the poem reached the Kremlin through an informer. In a sense the epigram to Stalin was a more serious – and successful – suicide attempt than his jump from the window in the psychiatric hospital in Cherdyn, after he had been imprisoned in the Lubyanka and sent into exile. This proved, as some suicide attempts do, therapeutic: as he says in 'Stanzas': 'A jump and I am back in my mind.'

He began to write again in April 1935, and the marvellous *Voronezh Notebooks* followed, expressing a love of life and concern for humanity. It was at Voronezh that he wrote the unstranslated 'Ode to Stalin', which is quite long, complex and far from adulatory. It was written down in a desperate attempt to save his wife and himself. At the end of his three year term of exile in Voronezh he lived briefly in Moscow, then Vaselovo and Kalinin, before his final arrest at a sanatorium in Samatikha on 1 May 1938. The Great Terror was at its height. Mandelstam was sentenced to five years' hard labour for counter-revolutionary activities. He died of 'heart failure' in a transit camp near Vladivostok in Eastern Siberia on 27 December 1938.

Nadezhda Mandelstam was his constant companion, his wife, helper, and his walking archive. It is due to her that his poems survive. In her books *Hope Against Hope* and *Hope Abandoned* she became the memoirist of his times, and the defender of faith of his poetry. Her determination, as well as Anna Akhmatova's, worked the miracle that continues through his poetry. Mandelstam has transcended the constraints of time and place which he so bitterly resisted. One hundred years after his birth, we can read, in English, his prophetic words: 'Yes, I am lying in the ground but my lips are moving.'

RICHARD McKANE
London, 1991

'The Moscow Notebooks': An Essay by Victor Krivulin

Moscow. Summer of 1917. A service of thanksgiving is in progress in the Uspensky Cathedral in the Kremlin: the patriarchate of All Russia, abolished by Peter the Great at the beginning of the 18th century, is being restored. The Petersburg period of Russian history had come to a close.

At the same time, by a strange coincidence, the Petersburg period in the life of the poet Osip Mandelstam drew to a close. Motivated by a sharp historical intuition, Mandelstam suddenly left his native city and appeared in Moscow, where he discovered the old Russia of before Peter the Great, which was unknown to him as a European and a child of St Petersburg.

His first meeting with the old capital came about when he was in love with Marina Tsvetayeva, with a light and pure love. Later, Tsvetayeva was to write in her memoirs, how in the course of those days she had 'made a gift of Moscow to Mandelstam'. Their walks together in the heart of ancient Muscovy, with its 'many-eyed cathedrals', were seen through the prism of the exalted admiration of the two poets for each other, though their own Moscow Golgotha lay in wait for both of them in the future. There were churches, full of people praying, the Asiatic, motley rows of stalls, and the stagnant silence of suburban blind alleys – all this seemed so unreal after swirling, revolutionary Petersburg.

But in the summer of 1917 forebodings as to what malevolent role the future Soviet 'whore Moscow' would play in the fate of the poet were drowned out by the sweet sound of bells which carried into Tsvetayeva's flat in the morning from the as yet undestroyed Church of Christ the Saviour. It seemed that the ancient city was living untouched by recent history, in blissful, prereflective ignorance of what was going on, in an atmosphere of Buddhist indifference to the increasing importance of the individual in the historical context. The paradox was that it was precisely this Buddhist Moscow which would itself turn in the 20s, into the centre of the new historic age, and into the symbol of a new epoch.

Mandelstam's first poems about Moscow, created at the end of the 1910s immerse us in a dreamlike reality of the present, penetrated by the past. The images of old Russian history find a meaning for the poet in precisely that historical moment when society as a whole, bewitched by the picture of the explosion of the revolution, spits on and tramples its own past in the name of the future. Mandelstam moves in opposition to the general flow and in the poems of 1917 turns to the most 'pitiful' episodes of Russian history, to the painful points of the nation's existence. So, in the poem 'On a straw laden sledge...' the complex chain of associations ties in the tragic fate of the murdered Tsarevich Dmitri and the heir, the Tsezarevich Alexey ('the whelp of Peter'), executed by his tyrant father, with the most recent victims of history. The poet foresees the possibility of these new victims so sharply, that the shooting of the tsar's family is seen as a natural and logical continuation, and the death of the poet himself is the finale, the full stop that ends the text.

At the end of the twenties, Osip Mandelstam and his wife Nadezhda settled in Moscow. The years of wandering round the Crimea, the Caucasus and the Ukraine were over. The poet did not want to return to Petersburg, which had lost its historical role as the capital of the empire. He chose the new spiritual centre of the new Russia. This was an attempt to accept the changes that were taking place, and to find an existential justification for them. It was a doomed attempt to find his own place in the new order of things.

Akhmatova was convinced that Mandelstam, by picking Moscow, had made a tragic mistake, which hastened his destruction. In Akhmatova's opinion, Nadezhda Yakovlevna, the wife of the poet, was partly responsible for this decision, since she couldn't accept his Petersburg friends and wasn't able to settle in his native city. But in the final analysis, this move was not simply about a choice of a different place to live, whether for psychological or material reasons – at the root of a matter was a radical spiritual reorientation and, even more, a doomed attempt to justify the advance of history.

Several contemporaries have left us with accounts which characterise the dominant mood of the Russian intelligentsia at the end of the twenties. Despite the fact that the regime was obviously getting crueller, those Russian intellectuals, who had been most vigorously anti-soviet and pro-western in the 20s, suddenly underwent a change of heart. The economic crisis in Europe and America somehow convinced them of the historical rightness of Bolshevism, and of the necessity not only of accepting the new order, but also of subordinating to it everything personal or 'subjective' ('the empty happiness of the few', in Pasternak's words).

Leningrad. December 1930. A last Petersburg cycle, completed after the Mandelstams' return to live in Moscow in January 1931, immediately precedes the Moscow Notebooks. It was here, in their first flat (if one doesn't count that of his parents') that his belated, hysterically desperate, but final, parting with his childhood occurred:

perhaps it was his way of settling of accounts with carefree infantilism – that eternal illness of the Russian intelligentsia, enchanted by rosy pictures of the wakening consciousness since the times of Leo Tolstoy.

No, it was with different memories that his Petersburg childhood returned of illnesses and hurts ('I've returned to my city of childhood illnesses and tears...' ['Leningrad', MN. I.9] about medicines ('cod liver oil of the street lamps on Leningrad's embankment'), of childish fears and phobias (oysters and guardsmen, in I.10). All this is recalled, of course, not without bitterness and regret that the torrent of time cannot be turned back, and always with a concentration on those dark, shadowy, detrimental aspects of what is first and foremost a highly intimate past, in order that it would be easier later to see the common, national-historic past as dark. He had to tear himself away from it, even if it cost him flesh and blood. For at the end of the twenties Mandelstam already realised clearly that to tear away his soul from the past was his only means of physical survival. The elemental attacks of 'Jewish terror', which were coming to life in the subconscious of the poet, not only forestalled, but also – and this can't be excluded – even provoked the intent stares of the 'unsleeping eyes' of the police critics following him. He had not yet been accused of bourgeois cosmopolitanism ('Mandelstam is a poet of the *grande bourgeoisie*': that was how his position was defined in an article on him in the *Literary Encyclopaedia*) in the crisis year for Soviet culture of 1932 but he was already hastening to justify himself by exclaiming: 'I was a child in the world of the powerful...' [MN. I.10] and further on in the same poem, almost tuning in the keen ear of his future persecutors to the notes they needed, he denied the very things that he would be accused of later:

I did not pose under the Egyptian portico of the bank,
self-importantly in a fur hat,
and the gypsy girl never ever danced for me, to the crackle
of 100 rouble notes beside the lemon yellow Neva.

Such a Petersburg should be consigned as a fossil to the depths of the memory, and lie there corpselike, like a deadened 'winter of the soul'. The poet tries to save himself from its 'minor' childish fever, suicidally throwing himself into the embraces of the unembraceable all-Russian chill, beyond which he seemed to feel some inhuman warmth.

so stuff me as you would stuff a hat into the sleeve
of the hot fur coat of the Siberian wasteland.
[MN. I.15]

Mandelstam felt that it was in Moscow that this inner national historical warmth was concentrated.

Moscow. Spring-summer 1931. The inner work on the reorientation of his conscience reaches a critical point. During these months Mandelstam attempted to carry through to the end a psychological operation on his past, on which depended not only his further existence in literature but also his very life. He did not succeed in this rescue attempt – fortunately for Russian poetry, but unfortunately for himself and those close to him.

Mandelstam returns in the Moscow Notebooks to the motif of 'the early times', although the subject matter is not so much childhood as a joint early 'season of life', where it is impossible to establish boundaries between boyhood, youth and student years. The best, purest and most festive things are subconsciously transferred from Petersburg onto Moscow soil, into another seemingly warmer and more favourable climate, into an atmosphere of spring and blossoming, of circus gaiety, music from booths, and simple enjoyment of the weather and seasons. The circus is presented as a joyful, risky, prototype of the youthful peoples' universe. (While I was reading Mandelstam's Moscow poems I kept remembering the 'circus' metaphors of Fellini's cinema, presumably because the childhood of the director coincided with the beginning of the thirties, and was spent in the tragico-farcical atmosphere of Fascist Italy, where the clown's booth (*8½* and *Amarcord*) travestied the mechanistic harmony of a new, totalitarian order.)

But here is Moscow in 1931:

> You'll say, 'Somewhere in the training square
> two clowns have settled in – Bim and Bom,'
> and the combs and little hammers start to play,
> now a harmonica is heard
> now a child playing
> a milky piano:
> Do-re-mi-fa
> and sol-fa-mi-re-do.
> [MN. I.25]

Intolerable scales, awkwardly played on an untuned *dacha* instrument, that tormented the ears and got on the nerves of most Russian literary figures – from Chekhov and Bunin, to Blok and Annensky, who inevitably touch on the *dacha* themes at the turn of the century. For them these sounds were inseparable from the suburban, Philistine, bourgeois way of life, whereas Mandelstam, reevaluating totally his attitude to the petty bourgeois (as his widow bears witness to in *Hope Against Hope* and *Hope Abandoned*), rehabilitating the 'little

15

man' cursed by Gorky, refuses to qualify as vulgar this immature cacophony. On the contrary the motif of apprenticeship takes on an almost warring, military character in the Moscow Notebooks. It wasn't only the clowns, who, like the foot soldiers, settled in on the training ground to learn jokingly the Pythagorean-Leibnizian music of the spheres, but the poet himself feels that he is a soldier and thus calls up to his aid new moral teachers (the intellectuals of the 1860s, the battling nihilists and the spiritual bomb-throwers, who traced their genealogy from Herzen and the scholarly Vissarion Belinsky with his apotheosis of the plebs [the fourth estate]):

> Don't complain!
>   Is this why the intelligentsia
> were downtrodden so that I could betray them now?
> We shall die like the foot soldiers,
> but we won't glorify the looting, the hired labour, or the lies.
>
> [MN. I.25]

Here Mandelstam was retreating to positions he had prepared for himself at the close of the 1920s, when his relationship with the Russian intellectual, populist Narodnik-orientated literary party went through a radical change – from fastidious rejection of it, a rejection which was widespread among the modernists at the beginning of the century (see Mandelstam's article on Blok, 'The Badger Hole', where he rebukes the author of the long poem 'Retribution' precisely for its provincial, schoolboyish acceptance of the 'back to the soil' movement of the Narodniks), through a cautious anti-aristocratism in 'Conversation about Dante', to the hysterical but hopelessly belated 'wonderful oath of allegiance to the fourth estate' in the poems of the last Moscow period.

Why the enthusiasm for the role of student? Why does this intentionally democratic 'morning of life', with its boyish aggression, provide for Mandelstam the most serious moral alternative to the everyday Soviet hell? And is it really alternatives that he is searching for as he repeats with a rare insistence in various ways the verbs 'to teach' and 'to learn'; he, who at the outset of his writing career in the 1910s had polemically denied any form of enlightenment and teaching:

> There's no need to talk about anything,
> nothing should be taught,
> and the dark soul of the beast
> is so sad and good...

However it didn't turn out to be that good: witness not only the terrible experience of the revolution and of civilian chaos, but also

16

Mandelstam's own experience of growing old. What can withstand such experience? According to Mandelstam it turns out that it can be only 'discipleship', understood here as the highest form of the revelation of the self, and as a purposeful inner movement, but one directed from without. But discipleship is a state that pertains to youth and it is obviously 'not of his age or rank' for the aging poet. It was as though he was tempted to coax and coerce himself to feel young. Time and again in the Moscow poems there are imperative exclamations, calls on himself (the existential analogue of the slogan forms of political mass propaganda, which were widespread at the end of the twenties and in the early thirties) as though the poet were agitating himself, persuading himself ordering himself:

> Get away! Don't ask for anything!

or

> That's enough sulking.

or

> Don't get excited: impatience is a luxury.

or

> Guess why you've given Tyutchev a dragonfly...

or

> (I) promise to build sturdy wooden frames...

or

> Keep my words forever...

The great majority of these examples, in an analysis of verb forms in late Mandelstam, convincingly demonstrate an overwhelming preference for verbs used in the imperative, referring as a rule to the lyric hero himself. Thus, the schoolboy persuades himself to sit down to the hateful school books. The poet, if he wants to survive in the conditions of the "cultural revolution", must, whatever happens, feel that he is learning, is an apprentice, or at worst a student. To survive, for the poet, means to "re-learn" (that is to forget part of what he knows from before), and only after that to 'learn'. To learn, so as to become a 'teacher of the (new) life', so as to have the full moral right to declare about himself [a later poem from the Voronezh Notebooks – tr.]:

> Yes, I am lying in the ground, but my lips are moving,
> and what I say every schoolboy will learn:
> the world is at its most curved on Red Square.

It is only with that consciousness of self that he can find a place worthy of him in the new society, which had passed at the end of the twenties from an infantile, pre-reflective, pre-revolutionary state to a state of juvenile aggression. In this society the teacher must feel that he himself is younger than his pupils, and indeed the concept of old age was taken as counter-revolutionary, and was subjected to moral and even legal discrimination, in the same way as, for instance, were the gentry or the merchant class. The young republic did not want to notice its old people, and if it did notice them, it was only didactically to juxtapose their powerlessness and conservatism with the living pyramids made up of young, trained bodies.

When it came down to it, during these years, the whole of old European culture was under suspicion – it had stopped being a social force, because it had proved itself incapable properly to secure the coming into being of the all-union festival of physical culture. But Mandelstam still lived on, thirsting to become young again, hoping for a 'second wind' which he should get any moment now 'on the race track', although he was now an old man, catastrophically balding (we should remember that even at the beginning of the twenties he had said in distress: 'A chill tickles my forehead / and I cannot admit immediately that time is cutting into me'). He was also suffering from asthma and heart disease, and, what was most dangerous in the circumstances, was bound by blood ties to the traditional European cultural values. (In that same year of 1931, Boris Pasternak discovered his second wind – he was able to adapt himself to the new conditions more successfully than Mandelstam.) However, Mandelstam's attempts to become young again were consciously doomed also for the reason that for the training ground where he tried out his endurance to find his youth anew, he chose the Faustian zone of European culture, or more accurately that creative 'longing for world culture', which he involuntarily associated with his own Acmeist youth. Unrestrainedly he filled the new Moscow poems to abundance not only with boats on ponds and rivers at holidaytime (that is the picture he creates of the park of 'Culture and Rest' on a Sunday, which used to be the Neskuchny Garden ['Neskuchny' means 'amusing' – tr.]) but also with heroic personages, transferred into the centre of the 'Soviet half-world' from the pages of school-books on the new European history of art – with Rembrandts and Mozarts, Raphaels, Titians and Schuberts.

> Raphael goes to visit Rembrandt,
> he and Mozart are in love with Moscow –
> [MN. I.25]

His Moscow, in paroxysms of extreme rejuvenation, was already claiming the role of the eternally young world capital of the arts.

The poet endows it with everything which once fired his imagination: the Paris pneumatic post, the 'oozing Black sea jellyfish', the woven baskets for Asti Spumante; he takes telephone calls with Polish accents; he rushes, as though to the tap of an oxygen tent, to the fresh air of the museums, concert halls and galleries. (A parallel with Pasternak may be drawn appropriately here: in the book *Second Birth* ['Ballad' – tr.] Chopin, as played by Heinrich Neuhaus, thunders out triumphantly over the garages and parking lots, demonstrating the eclectic inculcation of the highest forms of world culture into the new industrial way of life. Pasternak is sensible: he stops on this note, not falling into an ethical apologetics of the old culture; for him the artistic past of man remains a one-way street, and the moral imperatives which classical art was guided by are only acceptable in part and with limitations.)

Unlike Pasternak, the lonely and unestablished Mandelstam runs the risk again of immersing himself entirely in mankind's golden dream of Renaissance: we should remember Blok's diary entry about the early poems of Mandelstam: 'They are like dreams, but dreams exclusively from the field of history of culture.' But now the poet turns to old European culture in order to, having found his spiritual roots in the splendid past, feel himself equally rooted in contemporary life, and to become a man 'of the epoch of the Moscow clothes Co-op', but without burying his hope for a new Renaissance.

The spiritual, aesthetic searchings of the poet get closer, however paradoxically, to the general direction of Soviet art, which had experienced in the thirties a half-enforced, half-voluntary reorientation – from avant-garde to Neoclassicism and Renaissance styles (the flowering of Palladianism in architecture). These tendencies were to appear more powerfully later in the post-war years but they were being formulated at the same time when Mandelstam, in his Moscow Notebooks, was painstakingly trying to correlate the aesthetic pathos of mass sport spectacles with the Renaissance cult of the human body. The Pre-Raphaelite 'young men in Verona (who) raced in the fields' [MN. II.6] and the Boccaccio 'youths, who once swaggered about in skimpy green undershirts' [MN. II.7] and Dante's 'athletic discoi' [from Mandelstam's later Voronezh Notebooks – tr.], strikingly remind one of the 'Italianate' depictions of Soviet sportsmen on the mosaic and *al fresco* panels, which decorated in abundance the halls of the first stations of the Moscow metro, the proletarian palaces and the houses of culture. The atmosphere of the first Moscow Notebook, reverberating with the morning and emphatically spring-like, corresponds with the general emotional atmosphere of the worst official art: there are the same key images and emblems: the morning, the flowering gardens, youth, the water festival on the background of the immense colonnade (of the Tuscan order) crowned with red and blue flags. ('The chattering light of the [Moscow] river crests / speaks of culture, rest and water' [MN. II.1]). It is enough to compare the popular Soviet song of those years, 'The cool morning meets us' with some of Mandelstam's lines, such as: 'It's getting light now. The gardens rustle with the green telegraph' [MN. I.25] and 'I am conscious that the beautiful year thirty-one is blooming in cherry blossom' [MN. I.26] to feel both the resemblance in emotional colouring and the fundamental difference: Mandelstam never pronounces 'we' in a pathetically social context. At best he reluctantly squeezes out of himself not simply 'I', but 'And I', shifting as the danger hanging over his head intensifies, to a forced 'But I' [from the later Voronezh Notebooks]:

> But, like a peasant who's worked his private land
> goes into the state farm, I go into life and the people are good.

This is the formula, this is the final limit of his attempt to accept Soviet life.

Well 'every schoolboy' knows now how voluntarily the peasant who's worked his private land went into the *kolkhoz*. The attempt to join expressed through 'And I' became not enough in the thirties for a legalised place in Soviet culture, and Pasternak, for instance, feverishly having searched for a moral formula of appeasement of the spiritual structure of his own personality with the victorious social order, settles on a distressed guiltily apologetic expression of his poetic personality: 'But can it be that I (am not measured by the 5 year plan?)' and he is in the role of, a naughty child subject to stern reprimands, periodic slatings, but never to have his head cut off. So to the end of his days he was to remain a student, never successful at ideology, abused, but never thrown out of the class, because his spiritual kindred (Shakespeare, Goethe, Schiller, all translated by Pasternak) continue to occupy, in the invisible Soviet literary hierarchy, unattainably high positions.

Osip Mandelstam did not take the road of an apologetic person with a civilising mission, not because he didn't want to, but because he couldn't. He couldn't, above all, because of aesthetic reasons. Andrei Sinyavsky once defined his own differences with Soviet authorities as 'aesthetic, not political', and this can be applied to the aesthetic rebellion of Mandelstam with much greater justification than to the ideologised prose of Abram Terts. The category of 'beauty' becomes for the poet an ethical and only *then* a political reference point.

In his one and only direct political invective against Stalin [MN. II.20] (the fact of its discovery breaks off the Mandelstams' Moscow period of life, abruptly changes his fate, throwing him into 'the external darkness' of the Cherdyn, Voronezh and Kalinin exiles) Mandelstam accuses the 'leader of the peoples' in the first instance on the basis of aesthetic criteria: Stalin is not so much terrifying as loathsome and repugnantly deformed: 'his thick fingers are like worms...' his 'cockroach moustache' bristles... The General Secretary is like a caricature of an operetta villain, and his moral degeneracy comes from there – he is the desecration of all the laws of beauty and goodness. The new way of life is deformed, the principle itself of the new power is anti-aesthetic ('power is as disgusting as the hands of a barber'). Nature is disgusting amidst which this power is being realised: 'The earth is seething with worms' [from a Mandelstam poem of 1921 – tr.]. Even the new Moscow is made disgusting, for the features of the leader appear there in portraits: this city where the decaying breath of the East can be clearly sensed, where 'the rings of boulevards swoon in black pock-marks' and 'the rain-moist worms are plumper', where the 'captive bear cavorts, the eternal opponent (Menshevik) of nature itself' [MN. I.25].

This city lives as though under the anaesthetic of a new art, which deprives life of breathing. 'Cinema for us is the most important of all the arts' (Lenin's words), and Mandelstam likens the Soviet cinemas to opium dens, where the very air of existence is poisoned.

> The crowds come out dead,
> as though they have been chloroformed
> from the continuously overcrowded cinema.
> [MN. I.25]

Even before the revolution Mandelstam had a guarded attitude to the cinema, although the 'sentimental fever' of the first silent reels did not seem to portend the power of the screen over the soul and consciousness of the masses as it would be utilised from the end of the twenties for the purposes of political manipulation. The cinema, by democratically putting all those sitting in the hall on one level, subordinated the spectators to an extra-human force [from a later Mandelstam poem from the Voronezh Notebooks]:

> Even silent fish have words now,
> and the talking picture coming off
> the wet sheet of the screen
> approaches me, you and everyone.

Moscow. July 1932. The first sound-film theatre opened. For Osip Mandelstam this fact meant something more than just another technical innovation. The young Soviet culture had found its own words, and no longer needed the teaching voice of the poet. A year earlier, in the summer of 1931, Mandelstam had perceived the new life as silent – without speech. He saw his spiritual task in becoming the voice, the larynx, the throat of the epoch: based on this was his attempt to accept the 'Buddhist', pagan, abandoned to the East-of-the-soul Moscow, Russia and Europe.

> What a summer! The young workmen's Tartar backs are glistening.
> Women's kerchieves are wound round their necks.
> They have narrow, mysterious shoulder-blades,
> and childish collar-bones. Greetings
> to the mighty pagan backbone,
> which will carry us through a couple of centuries.
>
> [MN. I.29]

The roar of loudspeakers, deforming the normal human voice, did not only deafen the crowds herded into the claustrophobic, enclosed spaces, but also the poet, who stopped being able to hear his own voice, finding only in convulsive suicidal attempts ('a jump – and I am back in my mind') a shortlived sensation of the real connection with the world of the powerful.

[1990]

Translated by Richard McKane

FIRST
MOSCOW
NOTEBOOK

1. 'This life is terrifying'

This life is terrifying for the two of us,
my comrade, with the generous mouth.

Our black market tobacco is crumbly,
and you sit cracking nuts, my simple little friend.

One could whistle through life like a starling,
or eat it like your nut cake.

But – both of us know it's impossible.

[October 1930]

2. Armenia

Work appears to the people here,
like a menacing six-winged bull.
And the early winter roses bloom,
swollen with venous blood.

I

Armenia, you cradle the rose of Hafiz,
and nurse your brood of wild children.
Your breathing is the breathing of rough peasant churches,
with their octagonal, bullish shoulders.

Coloured with hoarse ochre,
you lie far over the mountain,
while all that is here is a transfer,
soaked free in a saucer of water.

II

A lion created the colours
you wanted, Armenia,
with a half dozen
crayons snatched from a pencil-box.

You are a country of pedlars' fires
and pottery thrown from dead mud plains,
you survived the red-bearded Persian and Turkish *sardars*
hidden within your stones and clay.

Far from the tridents and anchors of Petersburg
where the withered mainland sleeps.
You saw all those who loved life:
the rulers who loved executions.

Here when the women walk
with the grace of a lioness
and the simplicity of a child's drawing
my blood does not stir.

How I love your malevolent language,
your young tombs, where the letters
are like blacksmith's tongs,
and each word is an iron clamp.

[21 October 1930]

III

I can see nothing and my hearing has gone now,
I'm left with only the colours of terracotta red and hoarse ochre.

For some reason I started dreaming of morning in Armenia,
I thought: let's see how the titmouse lives in Erevan,

how the baker bends over and plays blind man's buff with the bread,
how he draws out the moist skins of bread from the oven.

O Erevan, Erevan! Did a bird draw you
or a lion colour you with a child's crayons?

O Erevan, Erevan! Not a city but a roasted nut.
I love the careen of your babbling streets.

I have dog-eared my muddled life like a Mullah his Koran,
I have frozen my time and shed no hot blood.

O Erevan, Erevan, I need nothing else,
I don't want your frozen grapes.

[16 October 1930]

IV

As time dawned you stood at the frontier of the world,
holding octagonal honeycombs in your hands.
You covered your mouth – a damp rose –
as you swallowed your tears.

You turned away in shame and mourning
from the long-bearded Eastern towns
and now you lie on a couch in the pedlar's stall
they take the death mask from your face.

[25 October 1930]

V

Wind a handkerchief round your hand and plunge boldly
into the depth of the crown-bearing sweetbriar
till the celluloid thorns crackle.
We'll get the rose without scissors.
But be careful that the sweetbriar doesn't fall apart –
rose dust – muslin – Solomon's petal,
useless for making sherbet,
giving neither rose oil nor perfume.

VI

A nation of screaming stones –
Armenia, Armenia!
Calling hoarse mountains to arms –
Armenia, Armenia!

Eternally flying towards the silver trumpets of Asia –
Armenia, Armenia!
Generously distributing the Persian coins of the sun –
Armenia, Armenia!

VII

Although the powerful circular forest has been chopped down it's
        not in ruins.
Stumps, anchors of felled oaks of a wild and fabled Christianity.
There are scrolls of stone cloth on capitols, pillaged from a pagan store,
grapes the size of doves' eggs, the flourish of rams' horns
and crested eagles, with owls' wings, still undefiled by Byzantium.

VIII

The rose is frozen in the snow:
snow six feet deep at Sevan...
The mountain fisherman dragged out his painted sky-blue sled,
whiskered snouts of well-fed trout
are on police duty
on the limy lake bed.

In Erevan and Echmiadzin
the huge mountain has drunk the whole atmosphere,
one should charm it with an ocarina,

28

tame it with Pan pipes,
so the snow would melt in its mouth.

Snow, snow, snow on rice paper,
the mountain floats towards my lips.
I feel cold. I'm happy...

IX

The villager's horse stumbles,
clattering over the purple granite,
and scrambling on the barren foundation
of the resounding stone of the state.

The Kurdish children run breathlessly
after the horse, with bundles of cheese,
reconciling God and the devil,
giving half to each.

[24 October 1930]

X

The fibrous music of water
is luxury to the poor village.
What is this sound? Is it spinning a warning?
Keep away from me. Danger is imminent.

In the labyrinth of the misty refrain
an oppressive darkness gurgles,
as though a water sprite
had come to visit an underground watchmaker.

[24 October 1930]

XI

I shall never see you again
short-sighted Armenian sky.
I shall never again squint and look at
this nomad's tent of Ararat.
I shall never open again,
in this library of clay authors,
this beautiful land's hollow book
that taught the first people.

XII

Blue sky and clay, clay and blue sky,
What more do you want? Just squint
like a short-sighted Shah over a turquoise ring,
over this book of resounding clay, over the land of the book,
over the poisonous book, over the precious clay,
with which we torture ourselves, as with music and the word.

[Tiflis, 5 November 1930]

3. 'Don't tell anyone'

Don't tell anyone –
forget all you saw
the bird, the old woman, the prison,
and anything else.

Or as the day approaches
and you part your lips
the shallow shudder of pine needles
will overwhelm you.

And you will remember a wasp at the summer-house,
a child's ink-stained pencil-box,
or the blueberries in the forest
that you never picked.

[Tiflis, October 1930]

4. 'The barbed speech of the Ararat gorge'

The Armenian language is a wild cat.
It is the barbed speech of the Ararat gorge,
the predatory language of clay-baked cities,
the speech of hungering mudbricks.

The short-sighted sky of the Shah,
a turquoise blind from birth,
will never read the hollow book
of clay fired with black blood.

[Tiflis, October 1930]

5. 'How I love this people'

How I love this people living taut under strain,
sleeping, screaming, giving birth,
this people nailed to the earth,
who think each year is a century.

Everything you hear from across
the frontier sounds good;
jaundice, jaundice, jaundice,
in the cursed, mustard undergrowth.

[Tiflis, October 1930]

6. 'The people howl like beasts'

The people howl like beasts,
and the beasts are sly like people.
The wonderful official who was travelling without money or papers,
was sent to do hard labour,
and he drank the Black Sea wine
in the reeking tavern on the road to Erzurum.

[Tiflis, November 1930]

7. 'The Armenian language is a wild cat'

The Armenian language is a wild cat,
that tortures me and scratches my ear.
If only I could lie on a broken-backed bed,
consumed by fever and the evil plague.

Spiders fall from the ceiling,
flies crawl over the sticky sheets.
Squadrons of long-legged birds are marching
across the yellow plain.

The official's face is terrifying as a gun –
there is no one more pitiful, more ridiculous –
despatched on a mission, shunted off
with no money or papers into the Armenian wasteland.

'Go to Hell,' they say,
to the old postmaster who stole the money,
the former guardsman who wipes the spit off his face.
'Get lost, and don't ever come back.'

A familiar hello thunders at the door,
'Is it you, old chap? What an insult!'
Shall we go on collecting deaths
as the village girl collects mushrooms?

We were individuals and became the faceless mass,
What is our fate to be? – who gave the orders? –
it is the fatal thudding in our chests,
and a bunch of Erzurum grapes.

[Tiflis, November 1930]

8. 'On watermarked police stationery'

On watermarked police stationery
the stars are alive.
The night has swallowed up the spiny sticklebacks.
The little office birds write their RAPP reports.

They like to sparkle so much –
all they have to do is put in an application –
and permission is always renewed
for twinkling, writing and decay.

[Tiflis, October 1930]

B

9. Leningrad

I've returned to my city of childhood illnesses and tears,
the city that I know like the veins on the back of my hand.

You've returned to it. Open wide, swallow quickly,
the cod liver oil of the street lamps on Leningrad's embankment.

Begin to know again December's short day,
when egg yolk is mixed with malevolent pitch.

I do not want to die yet, Petersburg! You still have
all my friends' telephone numbers.

Petersburg! I still have the addresses
from which I can find the voices of the dead.

I live up a back flight of stairs, and when they tear at the bell pull
the ringing hits me in the head.

I wait until dawn for the dear guests to arrive,
and each rattle of the slender door chain is like the clank of shackles.

[Leningrad, December 1930]

10. 'I was a child in the world of the powerful'

I was a child in the world of the powerful.
I was frightened of oysters and looked at guardsmen distrustfully.
I am not bound to it by even the tiniest fragment of my soul
no matter how much I once tormented myself to be part of it.

I did not pose under the Egyptian portico of the bank,
self-importantly in a fur hat,
and the gypsy girl never ever danced for me, to the crackle
of 100 rouble notes beside the lemon yellow Neva.

I took so much embarrassment, stress and grief
from the tender Europeanised beauties of my past,
and sensing future executions I escaped from the roar of revolution
to the Nereids by the Black Sea.

So why does this city have the right
to dominate my thoughts and feelings to this day?
Fires and frost have made it even more brazen,
arrogant, cursed, empty and youthful.

Is it because I once saw a children's picture
of Lady Godiva with her red mane of hair?
I still whisper to myself again and again:
'Farewell Lady Godiva, Godiva, it's all over...'

[January 1931]

11. 'Let's sit in the kitchen together'

Let's sit in the kitchen together,
smelling the sweet kerosene.

There is a sharp knife and a loaf of bread –
you could pump up the fuel stove,

or find some bits of string
to tie up the bundle before dawn,

so that we can go to the station
where no one can find us.

[January 1931]

12. 'Help me, O Lord, to live through this night'

Help me, O Lord, to live through this night.
I fear for life, for Your handmaiden.
Living in Petersburg is like sleeping in the grave.

[January 1931]

13. 'After midnight the heart steals'

After midnight the heart steals
forbidden silence from the hands.
It lives quietly, but is mischievous,
loves me, loves me not – it's not like anything else.

Loves me, loves me not, it understands, but can't catch me.
Why then does it tremble like an abandoned baby?
Why does the heart feast at midnight,
having taken a bite out of a silvery mouse?

[Moscow, March 1931]

14. 'Sherry brandy'

Ma voix aigre et fausse

I tell you absolutely
straight:
it's sheer raving and sherry brandy,
my angel.

There where Greeks saw
beauty,
squalor gaped at me from
black holes.

The Greeks took Helen
off across the sea,
but for me it's only bitter salt
on the lips.

Emptiness slaps me
in the mouth.
Poverty shoves me and says:
'Bugger off!'

Go on, do what you like,
who cares.
Angel Mary, drink your wine,
and never stop.

I'll tell you absolutely
straight:
it's sheer raving and sherry brandy,
my angel.

[Zoological Museum, Moscow, March 1931]

15. 'The Wolf'

I have forsaken my place at the feast of my fathers
and lost my happiness and even honour,
in order that future centuries may thunder with glory,
and that humanity may be noble.

This age of the wolfhound hurls itself on my shoulders,
but my blood's not the blood of a wolf,
so stuff me as you would stuff a hat into the sleeve
of the hot fur coat of the Siberian wasteland:

so I won't see the débris or the slushy mud,
or the bloodied bones strapped to the wheel,
so all through the night the blue polar foxes
will shine at me in their primeval beauty.

Take me off into the night where the Yenisey flows
and the pine tree reaches the stars;
my blood is not the blood of a wolf –
only an equal will kill me.

[17-28 March 1931]

16. 'It is night outside'

It is night outside. The deceit of the rich is all around.
It's 'après moi le déluge'.
And then what? The citizens will be hoarse,
and there'll be a crowd in the cloakroom.

Masked ball, wolfhound age.
Learn by heart the lesson:
stuff your hat up your sleeve,
and may God preserve you!

[March 1931]

17. 'Alexander Herzowitz'

Once upon a time there lived
a Jewish musician named Alexander Herzowitz.
He polished his Schubert
as if it were a sparkling jewel.

From morning till evening
he played incessantly
one eternal sonata
that he'd learned by heart.

Isn't it dark outside
Alexander Herzowitz?
Give it up Alexander Scherzowitz,
what's the use?

Let the Italian girl
fly after Schubert
on a narrow sledge
across the crunching snow.

We're not afraid to die
with the dove music,
and then to hang like a black
coat on the hook.

Alexander Heartsowitz,
it's all been played before.
Give it up Alexander Scherzowitz,
what's the use?

[27 March 1931]

18.   'Eyelashes sting with tears'

Eyelashes sting with tears as a sob wells up in the chest.
I sense the storm is imminent but I am not afraid.
Someone wonderful hurries me to forget something,
I feel I'm being smothered yet I want to live to the point of dying.

At the first sound I rise from the bunks,
looking around me with wild and sleepy eyes,
thus a prisoner in a rough coat sings a convict song
as the strip of dawn rises over the labour camp.

[March 1931]

40

19. 'I can't hide from the chaos'

I can't hide from the chaos
behind the Moscow cab driver's back –
I'm hanging on the tram strap of these terrible times,
and I don't know why I'm alive.

Let's take route A or route B
to see which one of us will die first.
The city huddles like a sparrow,
or rises like an airy cake,

and scarcely has time to threaten us from the street corners.
You do what you like, but I won't take risks.
Not all of us have gloves that are warm enough
to enable us to travel over the curves of whore Moscow.

[April 1931]

20. Untruth

With a smoking torch I go into
the hut to the six-toed untruth.
'Well, come on then, let me look at you.'
After all I too will have to lie in a pine coffin.

And she takes a pot of pickled mushrooms
out from under the bunks,
and gives me a piping-hot stew
of babies' umbilical cords.

'If I want,' she says, 'I'll give you some more,'
and I hardly dare breathe, and feel sick.
I rush to the door, but it's no good.
She grabs me and drags me back.

There are lice, moss and silence in the bedroom
jail of her remote hut.
'It's all right, you're fine...
I'm the same as you, old girl.'

[4 April 1931]

21. 'I drink to the military asters'

I drink to the military asters, to all that they blamed me for,
to aristocratic furs, to asthma, and to the spleen of the Petersburg day,

to the music of Haute Savoie pines, gasoline fumes on the Champs
        Elysées,
to roses inside a Rolls-Royce, to Parisian oil paintings.

I drink to the waves of the Bay of Biscay, to jugs of Alpine cream,
to the ginger arrogance of English women, and quinine water in
        distant colonies.

I raise a toast – but I still haven't decided which wine to drink –
the gay Asti Spumante or the sombre Château Neuf du Papes.

[11 April 1931]

22. The Grand Piano

The huge hall can scarcely breathe,
like the French revolutionary parliament deciding the fate of the
        opposition.
The bourgeoisie do not fight in the Gironde,
society is torn apart.

The shameful Goliath grand piano
is shamed by the discord
the lover of sounds, the mover of souls is
turned into a demagogue haranguing the crowd.

Master Henrik hops as if he were on a hobby horse,
his tail coat flapping.
Are my hands sledgehammers?
My ten fingers a little herd of horses!

If the world is to be made broader
and consequently more complex,
don't smear the keyboard
with a sweet potato.

There is a Nuremberg spring
which straightens out dead bones,
so that the gin-soaked sonata
should ooze like pitch from the vertebrae.

[16 April 1931]

23. 'Keep my words forever'

Keep my words forever, because of their aftertaste of sadness and
    smoke,
their resin of circling patience, and because my conscience laid the
    molten tar of work.
The water in ancient Russian wells must be black and sweet to the
    taste,
so that by Christmas the star would be reflected in it with all its seven
    fins.

In return for this, my father, my friend and coarse helper,
I, the unacknowledged brother, a splinter from the family tree,
promise to build sturdy wooden frames
for wells in which the Tartars will submerge the Russian princes.

If only these chilling executioner's blocks loved me!
Sticks are being thrown in the garden in a deadly game.
So for this I will wear a shirt of iron all my life,
and I shall find an axe in the forest for the beheadings beloved of
      the Tsar.

[3 May 1931]

24.   Canzone

Tomorrow will I really see
the hoarders of the mountain landscape,
the monopolists of granite?
The heart beats with glory.

The eagle-eyed professors,
Egyptologists and numismatists,
are sombre-crested birds
with their tough flesh and broad breasts.

Now Zeus with the golden fingers
of a cabinet-maker twiddles
the remarkable onion lenses,
the gift of the Psalmist to the seer.

He looks through the exquisite binoculars of Zeiss,
the expensive present from King David,
and sees all the wrinkles in the granite,
and a pine tree or a village as small as an insect.

I'll forsake the land of the Hyperboreans
to feast my eyes on the last act of fate.
I'll say 'This is for ever' to the Rabbi elder
for his crimson embrace.

The edge of unshaven mountains cannot be seen yet,
the scrub growth is prickly,
and, like a newly-washed fable,
the green valley is fresh and bitter.

I love the army binoculars
with their usurous magnification of vision.
The world has only two unfaded colours left:
the yellow of jealousy and the red of impatience.

[26 May 1931]

25. Midnight in Moscow

It is midnight in Moscow. The Buddhist summer is luxurious.
The streets disperse in a shallow staccato of pointed ironshod boots.
The rings of boulevards swoon in black pock-marks.
It's not calm in Moscow even at night,
as peace runs from under horses' hooves.
You'll say, 'Somewhere in the training square
two clowns have settled in – Bim and Bom,'
and the combs and little hammers start to play,
now a harmonica is heard
now a child playing
a milky piano:
Do-re-mi-fa
and sol-fa-mi-re-do.

There were times, when I was younger,
that I'd go out in a rubber mackintosh glued together,
into the broad splayed-out paws of the boulevards
where the gypsy's skinny ankles beat against her hem,
where the captive bear cavorts,
the eternal opponent of nature itself.
The scent of the cherry-laurel was overbearing.
Where are you going? There are no laurels or cherries...

I shall tighten the weight
of the fast running kitchen clock.
My God, this time is rough,
and yet I love to catch it by the tail.
It's not to blame for its own pace,
and yet it is a petty thief.

Get away! Don't ask for anything!
Don't complain!
                    Is this why the intelligentsia
were downtrodden so that I could betray them now?
We shall die like footsoldiers,
but we won't glorify the looting, the hired labour, or the lies.

When I die you will cover me
with our threadbare tartan blanket as if with a flag.
Let's drink, my little friend,
to the oatmeal dregs of our sad fate.

The crowds come out dead
as though they have been chloroformed
from the continuously overcrowded cinema.
How venous they are
and how much they need oxygen!

It's about time you knew, I too am a man of my time.
I live in the age of the Moscow Clothes Co-op.
Look how badly my jacket fits;
how I walk and talk.
If you tried to tear me from the age,
I swear you'd break your neck.

I talk with the epoch,
but does it really have the soul of a demagogue?
Has it lived off us as shamefully
as a wrinkled little beast in a Tibetan temple?
It scratches and is put in a tin bath.
'Let's have another drink, monkey.'

Although it is insulting you should know that
there is fornication in work, and it is in our blood.

It's getting light now. The gardens rustle with the green telegraph.
Raphael goes to visit Rembrandt,
he and Mozart are in love with Moscow –
for its hazel eyes, for the drunken banter of its sparrows.
The draughts are passed from flat to flat
as if on an aerial conveyor belt,
like the ooze of the Black Sea jellyfish,
or the pneumatic postal service,
like the hooligan students in May.

[May – 4 June 1931]

26.   'That's enough sulking'

That's enough sulking. Shove the papers in the desk drawer.
I am seized by a glorious devil,
as if the roots of my scalp
had been shampooed by François, in the Paris of my youth.

I'll bet that I'm not dead yet,
and, like a jockey, I'll stake my neck
that I can still play tricks
on the race track.

I am conscious that the beautiful year
thirty-one is blooming in cherry blossom,
that the rain-moist earthworms are plumper,
and all of Moscow is going sailing.

Don't get excited, impatience is a luxury.
I will gradually increase my speed,
Let's go out onto the track at a cool pace.
I have kept my distance.

[7 June 1931]

27. Fragments from Destroyed Poems

I

In the thirty-first year from the birth of the century
I returned, no, was forced
to return to Buddhist Moscow,
but before then I saw
rich Ararat with its Biblical tablecloth
and spent two hundred days in the Sabbath land
which is called Armenia.

If you want a drink, there is good water
from the Kurdish mineral spring Arzni.
the most honest water, sharp and metallic.

II

Now I love the Moscow laws,
now I don't long for the Arzni water –
in Moscow there's the laurel-cherry and the telephones
and the days are distinguished by executions.

III

When you feel you want to live, then smile
at the milk tinged with Buddhist blue,
and look at the Turkish drum,
as it rushes back from
a public funeral on a red hearse.
You will meet a cart carrying cushions,
and you will say 'Go home geese and swans!'

Don't focus, just click dear Kodak,
the eye is a lens in a bird at a banquet
and not a piece of glass. More light and shade!
More! More!
The retina is hungry...

IV

I am no longer a child.
                              You, grave,
don't dare to teach the hunchback. Be quiet!
I speak for everyone, and with such power,
so that the palate of the mouth would become the vault of the sky,
and the lips crack like pink clay.

[6 June 1931]

V

The tongue-bear lumbers clumsily
in the cave of the mouth. And from Psalmist
to Lenin: so that the palate of the mouth would become the vault
        of the sky,
so that the lips would crack like pink clay,
more, more...

28.   The Horse-cart Driver

On a high mountain pass
in the Moslem district
we sat down to feast with death,
knowing a fear we had only felt in dreams.

From nowhere appeared a horse-cart driver,
whose face was burned and wrinkled as a currant,
He was monosyllabic and sullen
like the devil's hired hand.

Then he grunted out 'cart' in Azerbaijani,
and clicked his tongue to get his horses going,
while he guarded his face from us
jealously, as if it were a rose or a toad.

Hiding his terrible features
behind a leather mask,
he whipped his horses,
off to somewhere, until their last gasp.

We were shoved back and forth
and couldn't get down the mountainside.
Horse carts flashed past,
wayside inns flashed past.

I came to with a jolt. 'Hey, friend, stop!'
Damn it, now I remember:
he is the Minister of the Black Death,
with his horses gone astray.

His disfigured destiny
drives us to the delight of his soul,
so that the bitter-sweet earth
could whirl endlessly like a merry-go-round.

There in Nagorno Karabakh,
in the predatory town Shusha
I experienced this terror,
which was born into my soul.

Forty thousand dead windows
look out at us from all sides
and the soulless shell of lives' work
is buried on the mountains.

The houses stripped shamelessly
stand pink in their nakedness,
and the blue-black plague of the sky
is barely visible.

        *   *   *

Tender calves
and frisky playful steers,
and like ships in ranks,
she buffaloes with male buffaloes,
and finally the priestly bulls.

Like a crowd of people
massing forward, causing the earth to burst
into sweat, the layered herd of cattle
sailed directly at us
like an armada in the dust.

[June 1931]

29.   'After having dipped one's little finger'

After having dipped one's little finger
in the Moscow river one can now
peel the transfer off the Robber Kremlin.
These pistachio green dovecotes are so beautiful
that one should scatter them millet or oats.
The Ivan the Great belltower
is a huge adolescent dunce, despite its age.
It should be sent abroad to finish
its education. But what's the use? It's a disgrace.

The whole town lies open before us:
the suburban gardens and the factories
whose four chimneys shroud the water with smoke
seem to be bathing in the Moscow river.
Having thrown back the rosewood top
of the thundering grand piano
that is Moscow, we will probe
into its sonorous insides.
White guardsmen haven't you seen or heard it?

It seems to me that our time, like any other time,
is illegal. As a young boy follows the grown-ups
into the wrinkled waters,
I will go into the future
and, it seems, I will not see it.

I'll never walk in step with the lads
into the regimented sports arenas.
I won't jump from my bed at dawn,
woken by the dispatch rider with my call-up papers,
and I will not, even as a shadow,
enter the nightmarish crystal palaces.

Every day I find it more difficult to breathe,
but meanwhile I cannot gamble for time.
Only the heart of man and horse
are born to enjoy the race.

Faust's banal and youthful devil
leaps on the old man's ribcage,
and suggests I go boating for an hour,
or walking on the Sparrow Hills
or whip round the city on a tram.
Moscow's busy. Today she's nanny,
fussing over her forty thousand charges in their cradles.
She's alone, spinning the thread of destiny.

*   *   *

What a summer! The young workmen's Tartar backs are glistening.
Women's kerchieves are wound round their necks.
They have narrow, mysterious shoulder-blades,
and childish collar-bones. Greetings
to the mighty pagan backbone,
which will carry us through a couple of centuries.

[July – August 1931]

30. 'I've many years to live'

I've many years to live before I'm a patriarch.
I'm at an age that commands little respect.
They swear at me, behind my back,
in the senseless, pointless language of tram fights.
'You bastard!' Well, I apologise,
but deep down I don't change at all.

When you think of your connection with the world
you can't believe it. It is nonsense.
A midnight key from someone else's flat,
a silver penny in the pocket,
and stolen film.

I hurl myself like a puppy at the hysterical
ringing of the telephone.
I hear greetings spoken in Polish,
a gentle long distance rebuke,
or an unfulfilled promise.

You're always thinking about what you really desire
in the midst of all the crackers and fireworks.
Then you burst, and all that's left
is confusion and being out of work.
Just try even getting a light for a cigarette from that.

I smile at times, at times I timidly dress up
and go out with my white-knobbed cane.
I listen to sonatas in the backstreets.
My mouth waters as I pass by food-stalls.
I leaf through books in muddy doorways,
and I'm not living but somehow I am.

I shall walk to the sparrows and the reporters
and the street photographers who will take my picture,
and in five minutes pull it out
like a wet spade from a child's bucket,
and I'll look at my likeness
against the backdrop of the purple Shah mountain.

Or I'll go on errands
into the steamy basement laundry
where the clean, honest Chinamen
eat fried dough balls with chopsticks
and play with narrow cut cards,
and drink vodka as the swallows sip the Yangtse.

I enter the robbers' paradise of museums
where Rembrandt paintings gleam
like rubbed Cordoba leather.
I'll gaze at the Titian priests in tricorn hats,
and wonder at Tintoretto's thousand squawking parrots.

And how much I want to be carried away by play,
to have a conversation, to speak the truth,
to blow my depression to the mist, the devil and to hell,
to take someone by the hand and say to him 'Be kind –
we're on the same road.'

[21 August – 19 October 1931]

SECOND
MOSCOW
NOTEBOOK

1. 'The factories, bathing in the Moscow river'

The factories, bathing in the Moscow river,
spin cotton; and the broad green gardens stretch alongside it.
The chattering light of the river crests
speaks of culture, rest and water.

The tubercular, foppish, bureaucratic river,
the Lenin hills, above the Neskuchny Gardens which are the boring
        consistency of halva,
are the stamps and postcards, which like ships
carry us now and into the future.

The Oka river has raised an eyebrow,
that's why there's a breeze on the Moscow river.
Her little sister Klyazma's eyelashes flutter,
that's why the ducks swim on the Yauza.

The Moscow river smells like post-office glue,
the bell-mouthed loudspeakers blare out Schubert.
The water is a spray of pinpoints, and the air
is more tender than the frog-skin of air balloons.

[May 1932]

2. 'O, how we love to play the hypocrite'

O, how we love to play the hypocrite,
and how easily we forget,
that in childhood we are nearer death
than in our mature years.

The child who has not slept well
still sucks his indignation from a saucer,
but I have no one to blame,
and wherever I go I'm alone.

The animals moult, the fish play
in the deep swoon of the waters.
O, if only I could be spared from seeing
the painful turns of human passions, human cares.

[May 1932]

3. Lamarck

There was an old man, a clumsy, timid patriarch,
who was as shy as a young boy.
Who was it who fought a duel for nature's honour?
Why, of course, it was fiery Lamarck.

If life is only a correction mark
on a short repossessed day,
then I will be on the last run
on Lamarck's moving ladder.

I'll descend to the worms and the vermin,
scuttling among lizards and snakes,
down the springy gangplank to nature's subdivisions
until I diminish and disappear like Proteus.

I'll become crustaceous,
and cold-blooded,
suckers will grow all over me,
and like a mollusc I will drink the foam of the ocean.

We went past the ranks of insects
with their full wine-glass eyes.
He said: 'Nature is all in chaos,
there's no vision left – you are seeing for the last time.'

He said, 'You've had enough rich harmony,
you loved Mozart in vain.
The spider's deafness is upon us,
the abyss is stronger than our powers.'

Nature has abandoned us,
as though she didn't need us,
and she laid a primeval brain
like a sword into a dark sheath.

She forgot the drawbridge,
it was too late to lower it,
for those who have a green grave,
red breathing, and buoyant laughter.

[7-9 May 1932]

4. 'When Russian gold'

When Russian gold
forced its way into far-off Korea
I ran off into the conservatory
holding an iris to my cheek.

It was the time of erupting laughter,
and swollen thyroid glands,
it was the time of Taras Bulba
and the approaching thunderstorm.

It was the time of decisions and self-will,
and the advance of the Trojan horse.
Over the log-pile was an embassy
of air, sun and fire.

The atmosphere from the bonfires
was thick as sticky crawling caterpillars.
And cheers resounded on the mountain of wood
at the news of Tsushima and of the fortress of St Peter and Paul.

God help us,
we went off, in our high boots,
to the mountain and young prince Chlor,
looking for chloroform.

I've outlived that adolescent,
and my path opens wide before me.
Now I've other dreams and other refuges,
but I'm still a bandit at heart.

[11-13 May 1932]

5. Impressionism

The artist has painted
the deep swoon of lilacs.
He has placed opaque scales on the canvas
which reverberate in steps of colour.

He understood the thick-baked
summeriness of oils,
heated by the lilac brain
to expand into closeness.

And the shadow, ever more lilac,
is it a whistle or a whip, dying like a match.
You'd say, 'the cooks in the kitchen
are preparing plump pigeons.'

You can just barely see a swing
and some veils,
and in the twilight fragmentation
the bumble bees have already settled.

[23 May 1932]

6. 'Remember how the young men'

Remember how the young men
in Verona
raced in the fields
striving to win the green banner.

But the runner in
Dante's book
will run arguments around them
and outrun them all.

[May 1932]

7. Novellino

Remember how Dante's
runners competed in
the spring for the honour
of the green trophy.

In their leather boots
they scattered over hills
and dark velvet meadows
like poppies by the roadside.

Don't mention those garrulous
vagrants, the Florentines to me.
They're a pack of incorrigible liars
and hired murderers.

As the church bells rang
they prayed in a drunken stupor.
They gave hawks as presents
to the Turkish sultan.

But, alas, the candles of the hot-headed
young bloods have burnt out;
those youths, who once swaggered about
in skimpy green undershirts,

who conquered their own guilt
and the plague's affliction
and served many,
different masters.

There's no one left to tell the story
of the women in their long, sinful dresses,
whose days passed like a dream
in ensnaring occupations.

They told fortunes with wax and spun silk
and taught parrots to speak
and let scoundrels into
their bedrooms for pleasure or profit.

[22 May 1932]

8.   'Guess why you've given'

Guess why you've given
Tyutchev a dragonfly,
and a rose to Venevitinov,
but the seal ring is not for anyone.

The soles of Baratynsky's boots
stir up the dust of ages
and he's been granted the seamless
pillowslips of clouds.

Lermontov, soaring free above us,
torments us,
and Fet's fat pencil
is always sick with asthma.

Khomyakov's beard
is preserved by God
to hang on a nail for ever
by the gates of Jerusalem.

[May – July 1932]

9. Batyushkov

Gentle Batyushkov lives with me
like an idler with a magic wand.
He walks down the side streets to Zamostye,
and sniffs a rose and sings of Zafna.

It seems as if we were never apart.
I bowed to him,
and squeezed his cold hand in his bright glove
with feverish envy.

He smiled. I could only thank him,
overcome as I was with embarrassment.
No one has ever had his nuances of tone,
nor his murmuring ebb and flow.

He, in his awkwardness, brought with him
our riches and our torment,
the noise of poetry, the bell of brotherhood,
and tears shed in harmony,

And he, who had mourned Tasso, answered me:
'I'm not yet used to praise,
my language was refreshed by a chance drink
of the wine of lyrics.'

Then raise your eyebrows in surprise
citizen and friend of citizens,
and pour your eternal dreams
like specimens of blood from glass to glass.

[18 June 1932]

10. Poem to Russian Poetry

I

Sit down Derzhavin, make yourself comfortable,
you are a sly fox,
and your yeast has not curdled
the Tartar kumiss.

Pass Yazykov the bottle
and give him a glass.
I love his grin,
the throbbing vein of his intoxication,
and his incandescent poetry.

The thunder lives in its rolling:
why should it concern itself with our troubles?
And the thunder delights in
the taste and colour of muscat
which it swallows with every peal.

Rain drops jump and gallop.
Hailstones race in a herd.
There is a city smell, the smell of a flood,
there is a smell that is neither jasmine,
nor dill, nor oak bark.

II

Moscow and its suburbs
started rustling and quivering
down to its roots,
like the trembling leaves of the fig tree.

The thunder rolls its cart
along the wooden roads,
and the cloudburst paces up and down
with the long lash of streaming rain.

The earth seems
to lean over obsequiously,
as the clouds troop out
in the soft shoes of the executioner.

The rain drops jump and gallop,
hailstones race in a herd.
There is the sweat of slaves, the hoofbeats of horses
and a rumour of trees.

III   *To S.A. Klychkov*

I fell in love with the beautiful
confusing forest, where trumps are clubs;
where there is a red pepper in a maple leaf
and a blue-black hedgehog in the pine needles.

There, pistachio voices
have grown silent on milk,
and when you want to crack them into song
there's no truth on the tongue.

In the forest lives a race of little people,
wearing acorn caps,
and they turn the bloodied white flesh of a squirrel
on the wheel of torture.

In the forest there is a bird's udder, sorrel,
and the peacock blast of pine branches,
confusion and grandeur
and darkness in the nutshell.

The wood-devils with tricorn hats
and long noses poke with their swords.
The executioners read books
by the samovar on coals.

c

A ripple of mushrooms
in the harness of light rain,
suddenly springs up at the edge of the forest
after having hidden for a time.

On the seventh wave the outcasts
gamble for no profit
The horses snort, the cards are marked –
whose side are you on? The breakdown has happened.

And as the trees rise up,
brother against brother, hurry to understand:
how crude they are,
how very good they are...

[3-7 June 1932]

11. To the German Language
for B.S. Kuzin

I destroy and contradict myself,
like a moth flying into a lamp's flame at midnight.
I want to go outside our language
because of everything that ties me to it for ever.

Between us there is praise without flattery,
and true friendship without pharisaism.
Let us study seriousness and honour
in the West in a foreign family.

Poetry, storms are useful to you!
I remember Kleist, the German officer.
Roses twined round the hilt of his sword,
and Ceres was always on his lips.

Long before Goethe had been heard of,
the Frankfurt elders yawned,
hymns were composed, and the horses pranced
like letters dancing on the page.

Friends, in what Valhalla
did we crack nuts together?
What freedom did we have,
and what landmarks have you put up for me?

Straight from the novelty
of the first pages of an almanac,
we vanished into the grave as into a wine cellar
for a glass of Moselle.

A foreign language will be my sanctuary;
as long before I dared to be born,
I was a letter, I was a line in a vineyard,
I was a book you dreamed.

When I slept without form or logic,
I was awoken by friendship as if by a gunshot.
God of the Nightingale, give me Pylades' fate,
or tear out my tongue – I don't need it.

God of the Nightingale, they still recruit me
for new plagues, for Seven Year massacres.
The sound has narrowed, the words hiss and mutiny,
but you are alive, and with you I'm at peace.

[8-12 August 1932]

12. 'Old Crimea'

It's a cold spring. The Crimea is starving and fearful
and as guilty as it was with Vrangel and the White Guard.
The patched rags are in tatters, the sheepdogs are in the yard,
and the smoke is biting and pungent as ever.

The views are hazy, it is as beautiful as ever.
The trees are in bud, swelling slightly,
and are the real outsiders, and the almond,
blossoming with yesterday's foolishness, arouses pity.

Nature can't recognise her own face:
the refugees from the Kuban and the Ukraine are nightmare shadows.
The hungry villagers in their felt slippers
guard the storehouse gates, never touching the locks.

[May 1933]

13. Ariosto

Ariosto, the most pleasant, intelligent man in the whole of Italy
has gone a little hoarse.
He loves to name all the fish,
and pepper the seas with the most wicked absurdity.

Like a musician with ten cymbals
he leads the complex plot about knightly scandals
hither and thither, forever breaking
the music of narration.

He uses the language of the cicadas which is a fascinating mixture
of Pushkinian sadness and Mediterranean arrogance.
He is an incorrigible liar, playing tricks on Orlando,
and shudders and changes completely.

He says to the sea: 'Roar without thought!'
And to the maiden on the rock: 'Lie down without a covering...'
Tell us some more, we have too little of you,
while we have blood in our veins, and roaring in our ears...

Ferrara, you're a harsh town of lizards; there is no soul in you.
If only you would produce such men more often.
While we have blood in our veins
hurry and tell the story once more from the beginning.

It's cold in Europe and dark in Italy.
Power is as disgusting as the hands of a barber.
He plays the great man with increasing skill and cunning,
smiling from the open window,

at the lamb on the mountain, the monk on a donkey,
at the duke's soldiers, slightly simple-minded
with wine, and plague, and garlic,
and at the child dozing under a net of blue flies.

And I love his furious leisure,
his bitter-sweet stream of consciousness.
I'm afraid to pry out of the double-hinged shell
the pearl made of beautiful twin layers of sound.

Dear Ariosto, perhaps this age will pass –
and we'll blend your Mediterranean and our Black Sea
together into one brotherly blue expanse.
We've been there too, and we have drunk mead.

[4-6 May 1933]

14. 'It's cold in Europe, and dark in Italy'

It's cold in Europe, and dark in Italy.
Power is as disgusting as the hands of a barber.
If only a wide window onto the Adriatic
could be quickly thrown open.

A bee buzzes over a musk rose,
a muscular grasshopper is in the southern wasteland,
the shoes of the winged horse are heavy,
and the sands of the hour-glass are golden.

He uses the language of the cicadas which is a fascinating mixture
of Pushkinian sadness and Mediterranean arrogance.
He lies bravely, like ivy
clinging everywhere, playing tricks on Orlando.

The sands of the hour glass are golden,
there is a muscular grasshopper in the southern wasteland,
and the broad-shouldered liar flies straight to the moon.

Dear Ariosto, embassy fox,
flowering fern, tall ship, agave,
you listened to the voices of the yellow birds on the moon,
and were a wise counsellor to the fish at court.

Ferrara, you are a rough city of lizards which has no soul.
The witches and judges of rough Ferrara
gave birth to such sons and kept them shackled.
The red-headed sun rose over the wild land.

We're amazed by the butcher's stall,
the child dozing under a net of blue flies,
the lamb on the mountain, the monk on the donkey,
by the duke's soldiers, slightly simple-minded
with wine, plague, and garlic,
and amazed by loss, fresh as the dawn.

[4-6 May 1933 / July 1935]

15. 'Don't tempt yourself with foreign languages'

Don't tempt yourself with foreign languages – try to forget them:
after all you won't be able to bite through glass with your teeth.

O, how tormenting is the flight of a strange bird's scream,
you pay a harsh penalty for illicit pleasures.

At the final parting a foreign name will not save
the dying body and the thinking, eternal mouth.

What if Ariosto and Tasso, who enchant us, who enchant us,
are monsters with blue brains and scaly, wet eyes.

In punishment for your arrogance, you incorrigible lover of sounds,
you'll receive the sponge soaked in vinegar for your treacherous lips.

16. 'The friend of Ariosto'

The friend of Ariosto, friend of Petrarch, Tasso's friend –
used the bitter-sweet stream of consciousness.
I'm afraid to pry out of the double-hinged shell
the pearl made of beautiful twin layers of sound.

17. 'The flat is quiet as paper'

The flat is quiet as paper,
empty, without any ornaments.
One can hear the moisture bubbling
in the radiators.

Everything is in order.
The phone sits still like a frozen frog.
Our possessions, who have seen it all,
want to be on the move again.

And the cursed walls are thin,
and there's nowhere left to run,
and I'm forced to entertain someone,
like a fool playing a comb.

More brazen than a Komsomol cell
more brazen than a student song,
I teach bird calls
to the executioners perched on the school bench.

I read rationed books,
and catch fragments of demagogue speeches,
and sing a menacing lullaby
to the child of the *kulak*.

Some realist writer,
comber of the collective farm's flax,
someone with blood in his ink
deserves such a hell.

After the purges are boiled away,
some honest traitor
is left like salt around the edges,
a good family man who will take a swipe at a moth like me.

How much torture and anger
is hidden in each veiled hint,
as though Nekrasov's hammer
were smashing in nails in my walls.

Come on now, it's time for you to put your head on the block,
you're seventy years old,
you slovenly old man,
it's time for you to put your boots on.

It's not the ancient spring of Hippocrene,
which will burst through the cardboard walls,
but the gush of age-old terror
which will flood this evil Moscow home.

[Furmanov backstreet, Moscow, November 1933]

18. 'Our sacred youth'

Our sacred youth
have good songs in their blood;
songs like lullabies
battle cries against feudal landlords.

But I watch over myself
and sing something like this:
rock a bye despots of collective farms
and lullaby the *kulak*'s child.

[November 1933]

19. 'The Tartars, Uzbeks and Nentsians'

The Tartars, Uzbeks and Nentsians,
all the Ukrainian people,
even the Volga Germans,
are waiting for their interpreters.

And perhaps at this very moment,
some Japanese is translating
me into Turkish,
and has penetrated deep into my soul.

[November 1933]

20. 'We are alive but no longer feel'

We are alive but no longer feel the land under our feet,
you can't hear what we say from ten steps away,

but when anyone half-starts a conversation
they mention the mountain man of the Kremlin.

His thick fingers are like worms,
his words ring as heavy weights.

His cockroach moustache laughs,
and the tops of his tall boots shine.

He is surrounded by his scrawny necked henchmen,
and plays with the services of non-entities.

Someone whistles, someone miaows and another whimpers,
he alone points at us and thunders.

He forges order after order like horseshoes,
hurling them at the groin, the forehead, the brow, the eye.

The broad-breasted boss from the Caucasus
savours each execution like an exquisite sweet.

[November 1933]

21. Octets

I

I love how the cloth appears,
when after two or three or
maybe even four gasps of air
an expansive sigh comes,

and space, drawing green forms
with the sweeping arcs of racing sailing boats
plays, half-asleep,
like a child that never knew the cradle.

II

I love how the cloth appears,
when after two or three or
maybe even four gasps of air
an expansive sigh comes,
I feel so good, so concentrated,
as the moment approaches
and suddenly, out of my mumblings
sounds fill out and stretch.

III

When you've destroyed all the rough drafts,
and you hold a sentence in your mind
steadfastly, without tedious references,
integral in inner darkness,
when that sentence stands up on its own,
opening its eyes, that were squinting in concentration,
then its relationship to the paper
is the same as that of the dome to the empty skies.

IV

O butterfly, O Moslem woman,
in your gaping shroud,
living and dying
so grandly.
You bite, and with your long antennae
you thrust your head into the burnous.
O shroud, unfurled like a flag.
Fold your wings. I'm afraid.

V

Schubert on the water and Mozart in the birds' chatter,
Goethe whistling on a twisting path,
and Hamlet, who paced his thoughts in fear,
all took the pulse of the crowd and trusted in it.

Perhaps the whisper was born before the lips,
the leaves circled and fell before the forest,
and those to whom we dedicate our experience
had acquired their qualities before the experience.

VI

Tell me, surveyor of the desert,
geometer of the Arabian sands,
is the unbridled freedom of lines
more powerful than the blowing wind?
'The tremble of his Jewish worries
doesn't concern me.
He creates experience from his babbling
and drinks babbling from experience.'

VII

The serrated leaves on the maple branch
bathe in the round corners of the sky,
and one could cover the walls with paintings
made of the colour flecks of butterflies.
There are mosques that are alive,
and I have just now realised:
perhaps we are the Cathedral of Haghia Sophia
with an infinite multitude of eyes.

VIII

The tiny attribute of sixth sense,
the eye in the crown of the lizard,
the monasteries of snails and shells,
the flickering little conversation of antennae:
the unobtainable is so close!
You cannot decipher or observe it,
as if a note had been pressed in your hand
that you must answer at once.

IX

Beyond the fossilised lessons of nature
the hard blue eye penetrates its law.
The rock plays the holy fool as the ore tears itself
from within the earth's crust, like a groan from the chest,
and the insentient foetus stretches
like a road, which bends into the shape of a horn,
trying to grasp the abundance of inner space
and the pledge of the petal and the dome.

X

We drink the delusion of causality,
from the fluted champagne glasses of the plague.
We hook onto magnitudes
small as an easy death.
The child keeps its silence
in face of the jumbled pile of pick-up-sticks.
The big universe sleeps in the cradle
rocked by the small eternity.

XI

I go out from space
into the overgrown garden of multitudes,
and pluck false constancy
and self-consciousness of causality.
In solitude,
I read your texts, infinity:
a wild leafless book of healing,
a book of problems with huge roots.

[May 1932 – July 1935]

22. 'The forest birds could tell of this'

'Valle che de' lamenti miei se' piena...'

The forest birds could tell of this,
the stream, swollen from salty tears,
the sensitive beasts and dumb fish
squeezed between two green banks.

The valley, full of promises and burning whispers,
the meandering curves of well-trodden paths,
the rock masses fossilised by the power of love,
and the cracks in the earth on the difficult slopes.

The firmest and most unshakable places are quaking,
and I am shaken. As though mourning is embedded
in the very granite in the nest of former happinesses.

Here I search for the traces of beauty and honour,
which have disappeared, like a hawk after it's torn its prey,
and left its body to lie in the earth's bed.

23. 'An orphaned nightingale sings'

'Quel rosignuol che si soave piagne...'

An orphaned nightingale sings
of its close family in the blue night,
and he melts the silence of the countryside
over the hills and valleys.

All night long he tickles me,
and alone for evermore accompanies me.
He traps me and snares me and compels me
to remember the death sweat of the goddess.

O, the iris of terror! The earth took
the ether of eyes that had looked into the depths of the atmosphere
into the blind cradle of dust and ashes.

The spinner's wish was fulfilled,
and I repeat as I cry: all the world's beauty
is less eternal than the flicker of an eyelash.

[December 1933 – January 1934]

24. 'My days have raced past'

'I di miel più legier che nessun cervo...'

My days have raced past like the sloping
run of deer. The time of happiness was briefer
than the flicker of an eyelash. Out of one final effort
I squeezed only a handful of the ashes of delight.

The heart sleeps in the crypt of the modest night,
at the mercy of grandiose delusions,
and presses into the boneless earth.
It seeks familiar focusses, and sweet intertwinings.

But what scarcely existed in her,
now having escaped upwards into the hearth of the azure sky,
can capture and wound as before.

And as I frown in consternation, I guess at
how beautiful she is, at what crowd she is with,
and at the storm of light folds swirling there.

25. 'When the earth sleeps'

'Or che 'l ciel e la terra e 'l vento face...'

When the earth sleeps, and the heat dies down,
and the swan's peace glides into the soul of beasts,
night circles with burning yarn,
and zephyrs sway the powerful waves:

I feel, burn, strain and cry: but she does not hear,
she's the same in her irrepressible closeness,
all night through I watch her,
and she breathes in her distant happiness as before.

The water speaks of a contradiction, though the spring is the same –
both hard and sweet:
is my darling two-faced in the same way?

A thousand times a day,
I amaze myself by dying in reality,
and rising again in the same extraordinary way.

26. 'As water flows'

As water flows from
one high mountain crevice, a contradiction to the taste,
both hard and sweet, two-faced,

so, to die in reality,
a thousand times a day, I shall be deprived
of the common freedom of breathing, and knowing there is a purpose.

27. 'You had blue eyes and a feverish brow'

You had blue eyes and a feverish brow.
The invigorating malice of the world attracted you.

And since you were endowed with magical powers
they decided never to judge or curse you.

They crowned you, but it was with the cap of the holy fool,
turquoise teacher, torturer, tyrant, jester.

You herded your words like a gaggle of ducks into Moscow,
a snowstorm, dense, impenetrable and luminous.

You are a collector of space, a fledgling graduate,
author, young goldfinch, student, little student, jester's bell...

skater and first son of an age that hurled you out by the scruff
of the neck onto the frosty dust of word spinning.

One often writes 'Execution', and means, 'Song':
perhaps simplicity is a sickness which can be wounded to death.

Honesty is not a toy gun pointed only at children,
it's not the paper that saves people, but the news.

As dragonflies, not touching the water, settle on reeds,
so the fat pencils swarmed round the dead man

Holding their sketch pads they drew for generations to come,
apologising to every line.

An icy bond is forming between you and this country,
so lie there and grow young, stretching into eternity,

and let the young generations of the future never ask:
'How do you feel there, you orphan, in your clean void?'

[10-11 January 1934]

28. 'A few random phrases keep haunting me'

A few random phrases keep haunting me.
All day I repeat: 'the richness of my sadness.'
Oh God, the dragonflies of death are black, and their eyes
are so blue, and the blue sky so absolutely black.

Where is the first-born's birthright, where is the joyful tradition?
Or the tiny hawk that floats in the depths of the eye?
Where is civility or the bitterness of deception?
Where is the clear figure? Or straight talk

complex as a skater's honest zigzags?
The skates flame blue:
do the blades whirl in the pull of dusty ice
clinking glasses with the hard, blue river?

The engraver's solution made from three different salts,
the voices of the wise German philosophers,
and the brilliant arguments of Russia's heirs,
made half a century into half an hour for him.

Suddenly the music staged an ambush,
no longer flying from the violin bows like birds of prey,
not for listening, nor for pleasure,
but flowing for the muscles and pounding temples.

It flows for the tender death mask, just removed,
for the plaster fingers which hold no pen,
for the swollen lips, and for the tight embrace
of coarse-grained peace and goodness.

       *   *   *

The fur of overcoats breathed. Shoulder pressed against shoulder.
Rude health boiled over – blood and sweat.
You sleep, enveloped in a dream in which you sought
to move forward half a step.

An engraver was in the crowd
offering to transfer onto pure copper
what the draftsman could only begin
as a charcoal sketch on paper.

I may hang on my own eyelashes,
ripening and swelling, acting out
all the parts in the play until I run.
The plot's the only thing we know today.

[January 1934]

29. 'When fate suddenly confronts'

When fate suddenly confronts
the timid, hastening soul,
it runs down the twisted path;
but death's road is not easy to follow.

It seems that he was shy of dying
with the appealing modesty of a novice,
or the first sound to echo round a brilliant gathering,
which flows into the linear forest of violin bows.

And so, the sound of the bow flows, on and back lazily,
measuring itself by the length of flax, by the length of filaments,
resinous, hardly believing that it flows
from nothing, from a thread, from darkness.

It flows for the tender death mask, just removed,
for the plaster fingers which hold no pen,
for the swollen lips, and for the tight embrace
of coarse-grained peace and goodness.

[January 1934]

30. 'Who died?'

Where was he brought from? Who? Who was it who died?
Where will they bury him? I'm not quite sure.
They say that some Gogol's died,
well not exactly Gogol, just some writer...a little Gogol duck.

The same bright, amusing man
who cultivated absurdity,
was absent-minded, couldn't grasp some things,
organised bedlam and hurled snowballs.

He's as silent as an oyster now. You cannot
get closer to him than a couple of yards – his guard of honour won't
          let you.
Something's being covered up for some reason.
.   .   .   .   .   . he just got confused and fell asleep.

[10 January 1934]

31. 'He conducted the Caucasus mountains'

He conducted the Caucasus mountains.
Waving his arms he went up the paths of the dense Alps,
and looking round, on the deserted shores
he walked, sensing the conversation of the huge crowd.

He brought across – as only a powerful man could have –
a crowd of minds, events and impressions.
Rachel looked for revelations in the mirror,
and Leah wove her wreath and sang.

[January 1934]

32. 'The Caucasus mountains'

The Caucasus mountains and the crowd of the tender Alps
that blocked the way, shouted to him,
His visionary footsteps mounted
the steep choruses of mountains of sound.

He brought across – as only a powerful man could have,
the burgeoning of European thought,
Rachel looked for revelations in the mirror,
and Leah wove her wreath and sang.

33. 'A bearded engraver'

A bearded engraver was already standing in the crowd, lost in thought.
A friend of copper and pine plates which are flooded
by three kinds of oxide until they gleam
and the surface of truth shines through the wax.

It was like hanging by my own eyelashes:
the air was crowded with winged angels from the paintings
of those masters, who put vision into faces
and order of the liturgy into crowds.

34. 'For Maria Petrovykh'

The expert mistress of guilty glances
who has such slender shoulders.
subdues the male's dangerous obstinacy,
and drowns his words.

The fish are fluttering their fins as they swim,
puffing out their gills. Take them,
mouthing their soundless 'O's,
feed them the half-bread of flesh.

We're not goldfish.
Ours is the fellowship of sisters,
the warm body's frail ribs,
and the vain sparkle of moist eyes.

The sweep of your eyebrows describes a dangerous path.
Am I really in love as a Turkish soldier
would be, with the vulnerable, red crescent
of your small capricious lips?

Don't be angry with me, dear Turkish woman,
I'll sew myself up in a sack with you,
swallowing your dark words,
drinking the crooked water for you.

You, Maria, are the help of those who are perishing.
One must anticipate death, and fall asleep.
I'm standing at your harsh threshold,
Go away. Please go now. Please stay.

[February 1934]

Notes

INTRODUCTION

1. *The Noise of Time*, translated by Clarence Brown (Quartet Encounter, new edition, 1985). Clarence Brown has also written a biography and commentary on the earlier poems, *Mandelstam* (Cambridge University Press, 1973).

2. Nadezhda Mandelstam: *Hope Against Hope*, p.232. Nadezhda Mandelstam's *Hope Against Hope* and *Hope Abandoned*, both translated by Max Hayward, were first published by Atheneum Publishers (USA) and by Harvill Press, and then in paperback by Penguin Books, and are now published by Collins Harvill. Osip Mandelstam's *Critical Prose and Letters*, edited by Jane Gary Harris, which includes the *Journey to Armenia*, was published by Ardis in 1979 and then by Collins Harvill in Britain in 1991.

ESSAY BY VICTOR KRIVULIN

'a jump and I am back in my mind': a quotation from 'Stanzas', written in Voronezh, after he had recovered from a suicide attempt in psychiatric hospital in Cherdyn, after a sleepless train journey with Nadezhda into exile from Moscow, where he had been held and interrogated in the Lubyanka. See Nadezhda Mandelstam's *Hope Against Hope* (Penguin/Collins Harvill editions, pp.68-89).

FIRST MOSCOW NOTEBOOK

1. This poem that broke the five year silence was written in September-October 1930, in Tiflis, Georgia, at the end of the Mandelstams' eight-month trip to Armenia, to his wife Nadezhda Yakovlevna, round about the time of her Name Day on 30 September. The nut pie is her "birthday" cake.

The Armenian Group: 2-8.

2. II. Mandelstam wrote in *Journey to Armenia*: 'The teeth of vision crumble and break up when you encounter Armenian churches for the first time' (*Critical Prose*, p.372).

II. l.5. 'pedlars'': *moskatelny* in the Russian, has a colourfulness in it, whether of paints or the colours of the Armenian terrain.

'sardars': Persian and Turkish rulers. In *Journey to Armenia*, Mandelstam says about a Persian pencil case: 'I wanted to smell its venerable musty panels which had served Sardar justice and the invoking of instantaneous sentences to put men's eyes out' (*Critical Prose*, p.356).

'young tombs': the Armenian massacres were only ten or fifteen years before the Mandelstams' visit to Armenia. See note to 'The Horse-cart Driver' (I. 28).

IV. On his death bed Pushkin asked for frozen grapes.

V. Rose oil was so valuable it was almost a currency.

VIII. Lake Sevan is a lake high in the mountains of Armenia that the Mandelstams visited. Echmiadzin has an ancient Armenian-Gregorian monastery near Erevan.

Ararat: from *Journey to Armenia*: 'I have cultivated a sixth sense in myself, an "Ararat" sense; I can feel the mountain's gravitational pull' (*Critical Prose*, p.372).

IX. Khardzhiev mentions that Mandelstam has in mind the Yezidic Kurds with their mixture of Christianity, Islam, and the ancient Iranian belief in the equal power of good and evil.

3. (Last stanza) from *Journey to Armenia*: 'Stupid vanity and sense of false pride held me back from berry-picking as a child, nor did I ever stoop to pick mushrooms. I preferred the Gothic pine cone and hypocritical acorns' (*Critical Prose*, p.355).

5. An earlier draft, quoted by I. Semenko, is helpful in establishing the meaning of 'mustard': 'But the lifeless plaster of the lands/ is a grey-green mustard poultice.'

'face like a gun': the Russian word is *tufyak*, traditionally translated as 'mattress', indicating flabbiness; however in Turkish and Farsi *tufek* or *tufang* are a gun.

8. 'RAPP reports': The powerful Russian Association of Proletarian Writers, disbanded in 1932.

The Leningrad Poems: 9-12.

9. 'dear guests': the NKVD (forerunners of the KGB).

12. Mandelstam concealed this poem from Nadezhda.

13. 'silvery mouse': A reference to Pushkin's poem 'Lines Written in a Sleepless Night': 'the mouselike scurrying of life'.

14. The epigraph *'Ma voix aigre et fausse'* comes from the Verlaine poem 'Sérènade' from his 1866 book *Poèmes Saturniens*: '(my mistress, hear) my bitter, false voice'. It is likely that Mandelstam's 'Angel Mary' refers both to Nadezhda Mandelstam and to Mary,

the singer in Pushkin's *Feast in the Time of the Plague*. 'sherry brandy' Mandelstam made up to mean 'nonsense'.

15. 'The Wolf': The Yenisey river in Siberia was also used, almost symbolically, by Anna Akhmatova in her *Requiem*. Despite Siberia's historical and contemporary associations with concentration camps it appeared to Mandelstam almost as a welcome refuge.

Fragments from 'The Wolf Cycle'

1

The newspaper spits up something that is not tobacco blood,
the girl taps but not with her knuckles –
the hot, disfigured, human mouth
is indignant and says 'no'...

2

...The monkish workers walked ahead
like mischievous children.
The blue polar foxes and the palaces and prisons,
only one powerful person sings...

3

The ink of the mud of Moscow turned to gold,
and a lorry grunted by the gates,
and the dense crowd, writing themselves into history
surged down the streets to the palaces and prisons.
[Reminscences of 1917]

4

But when I hear that voice, I shall go for an axe
and finish his story myself.

5

Be quiet! Never say anything to anyone –
time is singing there in the fire...

6

Be quiet! I no longer believe in anything:
I am a pedestrian just like you,
but your threatening, disfigured mouth
returns me to my shame.

7

Take me off into the night, where the Yenisey flows
and the tears on the eyelashes are ice,
My blood is not the blood of a wolf
and in me the man will not die.

Take me off into the night, where the Yenisey flows,
take away my pride and my work –
my blood is not the blood of a wolf
and others will come after me.

16. Nadezhda Mandelstam asserts this poem is in reaction to Pasternak's poem of 1931 (*Pasternak Collected Works* [in Russian] vol 1, (Michigan, 1961), p.341), and especially the lines: 'Rhyme is not an echo of a line/ but a ticket to hang one's coat in the cloakroom,/ a voucher for a place by the columns...'

17. The musician used to practise nextdoor to Mandelstam's brother's Moscow flat where the Mandelstams were staying temporarily.

18. Mandelstam was particularly fond of prison songs.

20. There was a rumour that Stalin had six toes (or fingers), but the main impulse of the poem is its almost folkloric horror. A rough draft fragment from the 'Wolf Cycle' links this poem with'The Wolf':

> Take me off into the night, where the Yenisey flows,
> to the six-toed untruth in the hut,
> because my blood is not the blood of a wolf,
> after all I too will have to lie in a pine coffin.

21. 'Asters': this is often translated as 'epaulettes'.

22. The poem deals partly with an unsuccessful concert by the pianist Heinrich Neuhaus.
Sweet potato, literally a sweet *'poire de terre'* or as Mandelstam commented impatiently 'just a frozen potato'.

23. In the last line Mandelstam is referring, as in II. 14. to Peter the Great.

24. 'Canzone': This poem is discussed in detail in 'The Power of Vision', in *Hope Abandoned* (Ch.35.x). The crimson embrace refers to the suffusion of red in Rembrandt's picture *Prodigal Son* in the Hermitage in Leningrad.

27. Included in these fragments were the lines 'and women's fingers smell of kerosene/ and blood spurts from kitchen sinks'.

28. The Russian word spelt in the text *araba* means 'of an Arab', but it is also a widespread Turkish/Azerbaijani word for 'horse cart'. In 1920 the Armenian population of Shusha in Nagorno Karabakh were massacred.

29. Last stanza: although there is a pencil note on the 'Vatican Codex' manuscript that this stanza should go here, and it is included in the body of the poems of the Merani Edition, Nadezhda Mandelstam goes on record in the Voronezh University Edition as saying: 'The Tartar backs are glistening': He [Mandelstam] rejected without any hesitation because of the last line. 'It's something completely different,' he said. To put it another way, the lads by the river for a first, touching moment appeared to him to be the basis of life, but he knew perfectly well that they were as slenderly connected to what was going on as himself.

30. In the most recent Soviet editions this stanza is included second from the end of the poem:

I love the squeaking tram trips
and the Astrakhan caviar of asphalt,
covered with straw matting,
reminiscent of the baskets of Asti Spumante
and the ostrich feathers of scaffolding
at the Lenin building sites.

SECOND MOSCOW NOTEBOOK

3. 'Lamarck': the French naturalist Jean Baptiste Lamarck. From Around the Naturalists in *Journey to Armenia*: 'Lamarck fought sword in hand for the honour of living nature...In Lamarck's reversed, descending movement down the ladder of living creatures, there is a greatness worthy of Dante. The lower forms of organic existence are the hell of humanity' (*Critical Prose*, p.366).
Grigory Freidin, in his book on Mandelstam, *A Coat of Many Colours* (Berkeley, 1988), advances the original and extraordinary idea that the 'moving ladder/staircase' is, subliminally perhaps, the escalator of the Moscow Underground that was being built at the time.

4. This poem is an integration of Mandelstam's boyhood years. It is remarkable for its concentration on heroic ventures or disasters, and its Eastern settings: Korea, Tsushima, Khlor, Troy, brought in via schoolbook writers Gogol (Taras Bulba), Homer and Derzhavin (Khlor). Tsushima was where the Russian fleet was defeated in the Russo-Japanese War in 1905. Derzhavin's Prince Khlor, in the poems 'Felitsa' and 'To Prince Khlor', is sent off by the Kirghiz Khan who has abducted him to find a rose without thorns. The first version of the opening line of the last stanza originally read: 'I have outlived the sicknesses of growing up'.

5. 'Impressionism': Jennifer Baines (p.58) mentions three paintings (all in Moscow art galleries which Mandelstam loved to visit – see 'The French' in his *Journey to Armenia*) that Mandelstam may have had in mind: Monet's *Lilas au soleil*, and Pissarro's *Boulevard Montmartre* and *Place du Théâtre Français, Printemps*.

6-7. Mandelstam in a theme of (his own) rejuvenation and craftiness is referring to the master, Brunetto Latini – Dante, end of *Inferno* canto XV.

8. The only mention of a dragonfly in the 19th century poet Tyutchev is the verse:

> In the stifling silent air,
> like the forewarning of a storm
> the rose's fragrance is hotter,
> the dragonfly's voice rings louder.

Alexander Pushkin (probable owner of the seal ring/talisman) was sacred to Mandelstam, a constant, but often unmentioned, presence and influence.

9. Zamostye is a town in Eastern Poland. Zafna: from Batyushkov's poem 'The Spring'. Batyushkov (1787-1855) became permanently insane in 1821. Torquato Tasso (1544-1595): Italian poet, to whom Batyushkov dedicated a poem.

10. Mandelstam was at this time much more involved with 19th and late 18th century Russian poetry (and his Italians) than with contemporary poetry. Despite his poverty in Moscow, he was able to collect many first editions of these poets, some of whom are mentioned in this poem and II.8. 'You know, if ever there was a golden age, it was the nineteenth century, only we didn't know.' Mandelstam to Nadezhda at the beginning of the thirties (*Hope Against Hope*, p.253).

11. Mandelstam met the biologist B.S. Kuzin, to whom this poem is dedicated, in Armenia. Kuzin loved German poetry, but argued with Mandelstam about this poem. Mandelstam was more drawn to conversations with scientists than with other poets at this time. In a letter (quoted by Khardzhiev) with the MS of *Journey to Armenia* Mandelstam wrote this accolade to Kuzin: 'My new prose is suffused with his personality, as is all this recent period of my work. I am indebted to him, and him alone for bringing into literature the period of the "mature Mandelstam".'

Christian Kleist (German officer in the original), Romantic poet, served in the Prussian army, died in the Seven Year War battle with the Russians at Kunserdorf. Pylades, Orestes' brother, is symbolic of friendship.

12. Old Crimea: variant 'the bullet-riddled views are still good'. The people, especially the refugees from the Kuban and the Ukraine, in Old Crimea after collectivisation and the failure of the First Five Year Plan were starved and in desperate straits. There, however, Mandelstam met Andrey Bely again, and wrote *Conversation about Dante*, and immersed himself in the Italian poets.

13. Ariosto (1474-1533), poet and author of *Orlando Furioso*, son of a judge, also carried out diplomatic missions for Ferrara.

14. This metaphor of throwing open a window has a parallel in Pushkin's 'Bronze Horseman', where Peter the Great (who is probably also the 'barber') declares his desire, that Petersburg be a window onto the West.

Mandelstam has described the agave in *Journey to Armenia* 'in the park the flowering agave [giant cactus] plants, like candles weighing six poods, shot up a couple of inches every day'.

'kept them shackled': Tasso was locked up in a mental hospital for seven years as a result of a court intrigue.

The last line 'We've been there too, and we have drunk mead', a quotation from Pushkin's *Ruslan and Ludmilla*, is perhaps like Alexander Pope's drinking 'deep of the Pierian (Delphic) spring.'

15. Mandelstam's cautionary (and guilty) poem to himself (and translators) on the foreign languages he loved.

17. Mandelstam's response to Pasternak's comment 'Now you've got a flat you can write poetry.'

Nekrasov: the socialistic poet of the 19th century.

Hippocrene: the classical spring created by Pegasus's hoof. Klyuev had written a dangerous poem 'the Revilers of Art', that both Akhmatova and Mandelstam knew: 'The wolf's jaws, the rack, the mines/ none of these could invent more treacherous tortures/ for the Russian Pegasus in the stone quarry.'

18. According to Nadezhda Mandelstam, Mandelstam kept mixing up *Bay* (feudal landlord – again a Turkish word) and *Pay* (boy). The *kulaks* were successfully collectivised, sent to labour camps or exterminated. The fact that *bay* (pronounced *bye*) is an integral part of a lullaby in Russian and English does not make it any easier for the translator.

20. 'Epigram to Stalin': Mandelstam read this poem to a number of people (not all together). One of them informed on him and it

reached the Kremlin with this couplet: 'You can only hear the mountain man of the Kremlin,/ the mass-murderer and peasant-slayer' from an earlier version. The epigram was his passport to exile – and death.

21. Octets. These poems, possibly part of a long work-to-be, on the subjects of composition, architecture, cognition, geology, evolution, and eternity stand out from the book for their taut structure. The 'fluted' glasses are, in the Russian, as sharp as needles, and again Mandelstam is harking back to Pushkin's *The Feast in the Time of the Plague*.

22-26. *The Petrarch Group*:

Mandelstam's versions of the Petrarchan Sonnets are Mandelstam poems in their own right, and we rightly place them in the *Moscow Notebooks*. They are from *Canzoniere*, CCCI: 22, CLXIV: 24; from *In Vita di Madonna Laura*; *La Morte di Madonna Laura*, CCCXI: 23 and CCCXIX: 25. 'In his versions of Petrarch's work Mandelstam strengthened the emotional force and removed a great deal of the "dolce" element' (Baines, p.100). There is a myth of Mandelstam reading Petrarch aloud round a campfire on his way to the Gulag.

27-33 *Requiem to Bely*:

Mandelstam also envisaged this group of poems as his own Requiem. 'Bely's death made him visualise the possibility that he would be thrown unceremoniously into a hole in the ground, with none of the last respects or funeral rites then being accorded to Bely.' (Baines, p.103). He had become friendly with Bely, the brilliant poet and prose writer, in 1933, when he was writing his *Talking About Dante*. Earlier he had criticised his Symbolist poetry. Much play is made in these Mandelstam poems on the word *gogol*, 'a black and white diving duck of the northern regions', leading into Gogol, and Vyacheslav Ivanov's nickname for Bely, 'Gogolyok', a little duck, or a little Gogol.

27. 'cap of the holy fool': a reference, according to Khardzhiev, to Bely's 1903 poem 'Eternal Call': 'The fool falls silent,/ full of joyous torments./ The madman's cap/ falls quietly to the floor.'

31. Victor Krivulin, in an epigraph he wrote to his poem 'Rapprochement', elucidates the first line of this poem to Bely: 'Witnesses of Andrei Bely's death told that in his last minutes of life, the poet clearly felt that he only had to stretch his hands out to touch the Caucasus mountains with his fingers.'

33. The engraver at the funeral was Favorsky, who illustrated the *Lay of Igor the Great* the early Russian epic, which was a favourite of Mandelstam's.

34. Anna Akhmatova gave the nickname 'The Turkish Woman' to this poem to Maria Petrovykh, a poet and translator she rated highly.

I am grateful for help with these notes to the Nadezhda Mandelstam books, to Jennifer Baines (for her book and conversations about Mandelstam at Oxford in the 60s), to I. Semenko's *The Poetics of Late Mandelstam* (Rome, 1986), especially for her discussion of variants, to the Struve Filipoff American Mandelstam Notes, to the notes of Khardzhiev in the very incomplete 1973 Biblioteka Edition of Osip Mandelstam, and to the Tallinn edition of Mandelstam 1989, edited by Pavel Nerler, which, although it has very few notes, includes all the later poems, and some variants; and for discussions with Peter Norman, Sir Dimitri Obolensky and with Russian friends, especially the poets Victor Krivulin, Dimitri Vedenyapin and Alla Gelich. The quotations from *Journey to Armenia* are from *Osip Mandelstam: Critical Prose and Letters*, edited by Jane Gary Harris (Collins Harvill, 1991).

When this book was already in proof, I managed to obtain copies of *Osip Mandelstam: Poems, Translations, Essays and Articles*, edited by G.G. Margelashvili and P.M. Nerler (Merani, Tiflis, 1990), and the more scholarly *Life and Art of Osip Mandelstam*, edited by S.S. Averintsev and P.M. Nerler and others (Voronezh University, 1990), which concentrates on *The Moscow Notebooks* and *The Voronezh Notebooks*, with commentary by Nadezhda Mandelstam and I. Semenko, and articles by various hands. It is a credit to Western scholars, and to the accuracy of the texts brought out of the Soviet Union, that there are no more than two dozen or so textual changes from the American Struve and Filipoff 1967 edition. These we were able to incorporate into our translation, and are happy that the publication of our edition of *The Moscow Notebooks* coincides so appositely with the large-scale publication of Osip Mandelstam's later poetry in his own country, and in his centenary year.   RMcK.

ALSO FROM BLOODAXE BOOKS

ANNA AKHMATOVA
Selected Poems

Translated by Richard McKane

'Akhmatova, along with Pasternak, Mandelstam and Tsvetayeva, is one of the absolutely indispensable poets of the century. We should be grateful to Richard McKane that such a generous, committed and well-presented selection of her work is now available in English' – DUNCAN TWEEDALE, *The Green Book*

'Richard McKane's long and arduous labour of love means that now these extraordinary poems are passed on to us in an English fresh and modern enough to make them sound as though written yesterday... This is indispensable reading' – MICHÈLE ROBERTS, *City Limits*

'This book is outstanding value for money. Apart from 264 pages of poems, there are notes by both writer and translator, an informative introduction and lengthy excerpts from Akhmatova's autobiographical writings. And of course the stamp of greatness is all over it; nobody could mistake the sound of someone creating on a different level. Reading these poems is like being higher up a mountain than people are meant to go; you can only take it for so long' – SHEENAGH PUGH, *Poetry Review*

'Whether epic or epigrammatic (and this new *Selected Poems* confirms how powerful she can be in either mood), she often expresses her sense of history by personifying it in one of the more statuesque and archetypal female modes of being: mourning, enduring, witnessing. In order to bear witness, she had to stay put, honing her gift to a tensile strength equal to any horror that war, famine or Stalin could devise... With so many of the later poems now in this one collection it is possible to trace the sweep of her development, and feel how the lovely early lyrics are balanced by the more tough and declarative pieces she wrote in her early seventies' – CAROL RUMENS, *Sunday Times*

'I read this book with increasing admiration... Last year was the centenary of Akhmatova's birth and this translation by Richard McKane, which is something more than a translation, is worthy of the event' – SIR JOHN LAWRENCE, *The Tablet*

'This taut, magnificent collection of her poems' – EDNA O'BRIEN, *The Observer* (Books of the Year)

For a complete catalogue of Bloodaxe titles, please write to:
**Bloodaxe Books Ltd, P.O. Box 1SN,
Newcastle upon Tyne NE99 1SN.**